THOUGHT-CULTURE

OR

PRACTICAL MENTAL TRAINING

THOUGHT-CULTURE
OR
PRACTICAL MENTAL TRAINING

By

WILLIAM WALKER ATKINSON

GYAN

Published by

Gyan Publishing House
5, Ansari Road
Daryaganj, New Delhi-110002
Phone: 011-47034999, 9811692060
E-mail: books@gyanbooks.com

Distribution Network
gyanbooks.com
India, USA, Canada, UK, Australia, France

ISBN : 978-81-212-6512-6 (PB)
First Published, 1909

2nd Impression 2022

Printed at: Gyan Press, Delhi.

THOUGHT-CULTURE OR PRACTICAL MENTAL TRAINING
Authors: WILLIAM WALKER ATKINSON

THOUGHT-CULTURE

OR

PRACTICAL MENTAL TRAINING

By WILLIAM WALKER ATKINSON

CONTENTS

CHAPTER I.

THE POWER OF THOUGHT

In other volumes of this series we have considered the operations of the human mind known as Will, Memory, etc. We now approach the consideration of those mental activities which are concerned with the phenomena of *thought*—those activities which we generally speak of as the operation of the intellect or reason.

What is thought? The answer is not an easy one, although we use the term familiarly almost every hour of our waking existence. The dictionaries define the term "Thought" as follows: "The act of thinking; the exercise of the mind in any way except sense and perception; serious consideration; deliberation; reflection; the power or faculty of thinking; the mental faculty of the mind; etc." This drives us back upon the term, "to think" which is defined as follows: "To occupy the mind on some subject; to have ideas; to revolve ideas in the mind; to cogitate; to reason; to exercise the power of thought; to have a succession of ideas or mental states; to perform any mental operation, whether of apprehension, judgment, or illation; to judge; to form a conclusion, to determine; etc."

Thought is an operation of the intellect. The intellect is: "that faculty of the human soul or mind by which it receives or comprehends the ideas communicated to it by the senses or by perception, or other means, as distinguished from the power to feel and to will; the power or faculty to perceive objects in their relations; the power to judge and comprehend; also the capacity for higher forms of knowledge as distinguished from the power to perceive and imagine."

When we say what we "think," we mean that we exercise the faculties whereby we compare and contrast certain things with other things, observing and noting their points of difference and agreement, then classifying them in accordance with these observed agreements and differences. In *thinking* we tend to classify the multitude of impressions received from the outside world, arranging thousands of objects into one general class, and other thousands into other general classes, and then sub-dividing these classes, until finally we have found mental pigeon-holes for every conceivable idea or impression. We then begin to make inferences and deductions regarding these ideas or impressions, working from the known to the unknown, from particulars to generalities, or from generalities to particulars, as the case may be.

It is this faculty or power of thought—this use of the intellect, that has brought man to his present high position in the world of living things. In his early days, man was a much weaker animal than those with whom he was brought into contact. The tigers, lions, bears, mammoths, and other ferocious beasts were much stronger, fiercer, and fleeter than man, and he was placed in a position so lacking of apparent equal chance of survival, that an observer would have unhesitatingly advanced the opinion that this weak, feeble, slow animal must soon surely perish in the struggle for existence, and that the "survival of the fittest" would soon cause him to vanish from the scene of the world's activities. And, so it would have been had he possessed no equipment other than those of the other animals; *viz.,* strength, natural weapons and speed. And yet man not only survived in spite of these disadvantages, but he has actually conquered, mastered and enslaved these other animals which seemed likely to work his destruction. Why? How?

This feeble animal called *man* had within him the elements of a new power—a power manifested in but a slight degree in the other animals. He possessed an intellect by which he was able to deduce, compare, infer—reason.

His lack of natural weapons he overcame by borrowing the idea of the tooth and claw of the other animals, imitating them in flint and shaping them into spears; borrowing the trunk of the elephant and the paw of the tiger, and reproducing their blow-striking qualities in his wooden club. Not only this but he took lessons from the supple limbs and branches of the trees, and copied the principle in his bow, in order to project its minature spear, his arrow. He sheltered himself, his mate and his young, from the fury of the storm, first by caves and afterwards by rude houses, built in inaccessible places, reached only by means of crude ladders, bridges, or climbing poles. He built doors for his habitations, to protect himself from the attacks of these wild enemies—he heaped stones at the mouth of his caves to keep them out. He placed great boulders on cliffs that he might topple them down on the approaching foe. He learned to hurl rocks with sure aim with his strong arm. He copied the floating log, and built his first rude rafts, and then evolved the hollowed canoe. He used the skins of animals to keep him warm—their tendons for his bowstrings. He learned the advantages of cooperation and combined effort, and thus formed the first rudiments of society and social life. And finally—man's first great discovery—he found the art of fire making.

As a writer has said: "For some hundreds of years, upon the general plane of self-consciousness, an ascent, to the human eye gradual but from the point of view of cosmic evolution rapid, has been made. In a race large-brained, walking-erect, gregarious, brutal, but king of all other brutes, man in appearance but not in fact, was from the highest simple-consciousness born the basic human faculty, self-consciousness and its twin, language. From these and what went with these, through suffering, toil and war; through bestiality, savagery, barbarism; through slavery, greed, effort, through conquests infinite, through defeats overwhelming, through struggle unending; through ages of aimless semi-brutal existence, through subsistence on berries and roots; through the use of the casually found stone or stick; through life in deep forests, with nuts and seeds, and on the shores of waters with mollusks, crustaceans and fish for food; through that greatest, perhaps, of human victories, the domestication and subjugation of fire; through the invention and art of bow and arrow; through the training of animals and the breaking of them to labor; through the long learning which led to the cultivation of the soil; through the adobe brick and the building of houses therefrom; through the smelting of metals and the slow birth of the arts which rest upon these; through the slow making of alphabets and the evolution of the written work; in short, through thousands of centuries of human life, of human aspiration, of human growth, sprang the world of men and women as it stands before us and within us today with all its achievements and possessions."

The great difference between thought as we find it in man, and its forms among the lower animals lies in what psychologists have called "progressive thought." The animals advance but little in their thinking processes but rest content with those of their ancestors —their thought seems to have become set or crystallized during the process of their evolution. The birds, mammals and the insects vary but little in their mental processes from their ancestors of many thousand years ago. They build their nests, or dens, in almost precisely the same manner as did their progenitors in the stone-age. But man has slowly but steadily progressed, in spite of temporary set-backs and failures. He has endeavored to progress and improve. Those tribes which fell back in regard to mental progress and advancement, have been left behind in the race, and in many cases have become extinct. The great natural law of the "survival of the fittest" has steadily operated in the life of the race. The "fittest" were those best adapted to grapple with and overcome the obstacles of their environment, and these obstacles were best overcome by the use of the intellect. Those tribes and those individuals whose intellect was active, tended to survive where others perished, and consequently they were able to transmit their intellectual quality to their descendants.

Halleck says: "Nature is constantly using her power to kill off the thoughtless, or to cripple them in life's race. She is determined that only the fittest and the descendants of the fittest shall survive. By the 'fittest' she means those who have thought and whose ancestors have thought and profited thereby. Geologists tell us that ages ago there lived in England bears, tigers, elephants, lions and many other powerful and fierce animals. There was living contemporaneous with them a much weaker animal, that had neither the claws, the strength, nor the speed of the tiger. In fact this human being was almost defenceless. Had a being from another planet been asked to prophesy, he would undoubtedly have said that this helpless animal would be the first to be exterminated. And yet every one of those fierce creatures succumbed either to the change of climate, or to man's inferior strength. The reason was that man had one resource denied to the animals—the power of progressive thought. The land sank, the sea cut off England from the mainland, the climate changed, and even the strongest animals were helpless. But man changed his clothing with the changing climate. He made fires; he built a retreat to keep off death by cold. He thought out means to kill or to subdue the strongest animals. Had the lions, tigers or bears the power of progressive thought, they could have combined, and it would have been possible for them to exterminate man before he reached the civilized stage. . . . Man no longer sleeps in caves. The smoke no longer fills his home or finds its way out through the chinks in the walls or a hole in the roof. In traveling, he is no longer restricted to his feet or even to horses. For all this improvement man is indebted to *thought*. That has harnessed the very vibrations of the ether to do his bidding."

And thus we see that man owes his present place on earth to his Thought-Culture. And, it certainly behooves us to closely consider and study the methods and processes whereby each and every man may cultivate and develop the wondrous faculties of the mind which are employed in the processes of Thought. The faculties of the Mind, like the muscles of the body, may be developed, trained and cultivated. The process of such mental development is called "THOUGHT-CULTURE," and forms the subject of this book.

CHAPTER II.

THE NATURE OF THOUGHT

It was formerly considered necessary for all books on the subject of thought to begin by a recital of the metaphysical conceptions regarding the nature and "thingness" of Mind. The student was led through many pages and endless speculation regarding the metaphysical theories regarding the origin and inner nature of Mind which, so far from establishing a fixed and definite explanation in his mind, rather tended toward confusing him and giving him the idea that psychology was of necessity a speculative science lacking the firm practical basis possessed by other branches of science. In the end, in the words of old Omar, he "came out the door through which he went."

But this tendency has been overcome of late years, and writers on the subject pass by all metaphysical conceptions regarding the nature of Mind, and usually begin by plunging at once into the real business of psychology—

the business of the practical study of the mechanism and activities of the mind itself. As some writer has said, psychology has no more concern with the solution of the eternal riddle of "What is Mind?" than physics with the twin-riddle of "What is Matter?" Both riddles, and their answers, belong to entirely different branches and fields of thought than those concerned with their laws of operation and principles of activity. As Halleck says: "Psychology studies the phenomena of mind, just as physics investigates those of matter." And, likewise, just as the science of physics holds true in spite of the varying and changing conceptions regarding the nature of matter, so does the science of psychology hold true in spite of the varying and changing conceptions regarding the nature of Mind.

Halleck has well said: "If a materialist should hold that the mind was nothing but the brain, and that the brain was a vast aggregation of molecular sheep herding together in various ways, his hypothesis would not change the fact that sensation must precede perception, memory and thought; nor would the laws of the association of ideas be changed, nor would the fact that interest and repetition aid memory cease to hold good. The man who thought his mind was a collection of little cells would dream, imagine, think and feel; so also would he who believed his mind to be immaterial. It is very fortunate that the same mental phenomena occur, no matter what theory is adopted. Those who like to study the puzzles as to what mind and matter really are must go to metaphysics. Should we ever find that salt, arsenic and all things else are the same substance with a different molecular arrangement, we should still not use them interchangeably."

For the purposes of the study of practical psychology, we may as well lay aside, if even for the moment, our pet metaphysical conceptions and act as if we knew nothing of the essential nature of Mind (and indeed Science in truth does *not* know), and confine ourselves to the phenomena and manifestations of Mind which, after all, is the only way in which and by which we can know anything at all about it. As Brooks says: "The mind can be defined only by its activities and manifestations. In order to obtain a definition of the mind, therefore, we must observe and determine its various forms of activity. These activities, classified under a few general heads and predicated of the unseen something which manifests them, will give us a definition of mind."

The act of consciousness determines the existence of Mind in the person experiencing it. No one can be conscious of thought and, at the same time, deny the existence of mind within himself. For the very act of denial, in itself, is a manifestation of thought and consequently an assertion of the existence of mind. One may assert the axiom: "I think, therefore, I have a mind;" but he is denied the privilege of arguing: "I think, therefore, I have no mind." The mind has an ultimate and final knowledge of its own existence.

The older view of Mind is that it is a something higher than matter which it uses for its manifestation. It was held to be unknowable in itself and to be studied only through its manifestations. It was supposed to involve itself, to become involved, in some way in matter and to there manifest itself in an infinitude of forms, degrees, and variations.

The materialistic view, which arose into prominence in the middle of the Nineteenth Century, held, on the contrary, that Mind was merely an activity or property of Matter—a function of matter akin to extension and motion. Huxley, voicing this conception said: "We have no knowledge of any thinking substance apart from an extended substance. . . We shall, sooner or later, arrive at a mechanical equivalent of consciousness, just as we have arrived at a mechanical equivalent of heat." But, Huxley, himself, was afterwards constrained to acknowledge that: "How it is that anything so remarkable as a state of consciousness comes about by the result of irritating nervous tissue, is just as unaccountable as the appearance of the *jinnee* when Aladdin rubbed his lamp."

The most advanced authorities of the day, are inclined to the opinion that both Matter and Mind are both differing aspects of some one fundamental Something; or, as some of the closest thinkers state it, both are probably two apparently differing manifestations or emanations of an Underlying Something which, as Spencer says: "transcends not only our reason but also our imagination." The study of philosophy and metaphysics serves an important purpose in showing us *how much we do not know*, and why we do not know—also in showing us the fallacy of many things we had thought we did know—but when it comes to telling us the real "why," actual cause, or essential nature of *anything*, it is largely a disappointment to those who seek fundamental truths and ultimate reasons. It is much more comfortable to "abjure the 'Why' and seek the 'How' "—if we can.

Many psychologists classify the activities of the mind into three general divisions; *viz.*, (1) Thinking; (2) Willing; (3) Feeling. These divisions, which result from what is known as "the tri-logical classification," were first distinctly enunciated by Upham although Kant had intimated it very plainly. For many years before the favored division was but two-fold the line of division being between the *cognitive*, or knowing, activities, and the *conative*, or acting, activities, generally known as the Understanding and the Will, respectively. It took a long time before the authorities would formally recognize the great field of the Feelings as forming a class by themselves and ranking with the Understanding and the Will. There are certain sub-divisions and shadings, which we shall notice as we proceed, some of which are more or less complex, and which seem to shade into others. The student is cautioned against conceiving of the mind as a thing having several compartments or distinct divisions. The classification does not indicate this and is only intended as a convenience in analyzing and studying the mental activities and operations. The "I" which feels, thinks and acts is the same—one entity.

As Brooks well says: "The mind is a self-conscious activity and not a mere passivity; it is a centre of spiritual forces, all resting in the background of the ego. As a centre of forces, it stands related to the forces of the material and spiritual universe and is acted upon through its susceptibilities by those forces. As a spiritual activity, it takes the impressions derived from those forces, works them up into the organic growth of itself, converts them into conscious knowledge and uses these products as means to set other forces into activity and produce new results. Standing above nature and superior to its surroundings, it nevertheless feeds upon nature, as we may say, and transforms material influences into spiritual facts akin to its own nature. Related to the natural world and apparently originating from it, it yet rises above this natural world and, with the crown of freedom upon its brow, rules the natural obedient to its will.''

In this book, while we shall fully and unquestionably recognize the ''tri-logical classification'' of the activities of the Mind into the divisions of Thinking, Willing and Feeling, respectively, nevertheless, we shall, for convenience, use the term ''Thought'' in its broadest, widest and most general sense, as: ''The power or faculty of thinking; the mental faculty; the mind,'' rather than in its narrower and particular sense of: ''the understanding or cognitive faculty of the mind.'' Accordingly, we shall include the cultivation of the mental activities known as Attention, Perception, Imagination, etc., together with the strictly cognitive faculties, under the general term of Thought-Culture.

CHAPTER III.

PHASES OF THOUGHT

We have seen that the Mind is that something within us which Thinks, Feels and Wills. There are various phases of these three forms of activity. These phases have often been called "the faculties of the mind," although many authorities decry the use of this term, holding that it gives an impression of *several parts or divisions* of the mind, separate and distinct from each other, whereas these phases are merely the several *powers or forms of activity* of the Mind. Every manifestation of mental activity falls under one of the three before-mentioned general forms, i. e., Thinking, Feeling and Willing, respectively. Every manifestation of mental activity is either that of the Intellect, the Feelings, or the Will. Let us consider the first of these three general forms of mental activity—the Intellect.

The *Intellect* is defined as: "That faculty or phase of the human mind by which it receives or comprehends the ideas communicated to it by the senses or by perception, or other means, as distinguished from the power to feel and to will; the power or faculty to perceive objects in their relations; the power to judge and comprehend; also the capacity for higher forms of knowledge as distinguished from the power to perceive and imagine." The term itself is derived from the Latin term *intellectus,* the primary meaning of which is "to choose between," which primary meaning will give the true essential meaning of the term in its present usage; namely, the faculty or phase of the mind by which we "choose between" things or by which we *decide.*

The phase or faculty of Intellect concerns itself with Thinking, in the particular and narrower sense of that term. Its products are *thoughts, mental images* and *ideas.* An *idea* or *mental image* is a mental conception of anything, as for instance our conception which we express by the terms, *man, animal, house, etc.* Sometimes the word *idea* is used to express merely the abstract or generalized conception of the thing, as, for instance, *Man* in the sense of "all men;" while *mental image* is used in the sense of the mental conception of some one particular thing, as a "*a man;*" it being held that no mental image can be had of a generalization. A *thought* is held to be a mental product arising from a combination of two or more ideas or mental images, as for instance: "A horse is an animal;" "a man is a biped;" etc.

The Intellect is held to embrace and include a number of minor phases or faculties, such as Perception, Understanding, Imagination, Memory, Reason and Intuition, which are explained as follows:

Perception is that faculty of the Mind which interprets the material presented to it by the senses. It is the power whereby we gain our knowledge of the external world, as reported to us by the channels of sense. Through Perception we are able to form ideas and mental images, which in turn lead to thoughts. The objects of which we become conscious through Perception are called *percepts,* which form the bases of what we call *concepts,* or ideas.

Understanding is that faculty of the Mind by the means of which we are able intelligently to compare the objects presented to it by Perception, and by which we separate them into parts by analysis, or to combine them into greater classes, or wholes, by synthesis. It produces ideas, both abstract and general; also concepts of truths, laws, principles, causes, etc. There are several sub-phases of Understanding, which are known as: Abstraction, Conception or Generalization, or Judgment and Reasoning, respectively, which are explained as follows:

Abstraction is that faculty of the Mind which enables it to abstract, or draw off, and consider apart from an object, a particular *quality* or *property* of an object, thus making of the quality or property a distinct object of thought apart from the original object. Thus are the *abstract ideas* of *sweetness, color, hardness, courage, beauty,* etc., which we have abstracted or *drawn off* from their original associations, either for the purpose of putting them out of sight and consideration, or else to view and consider them by themselves. No one ever tasted "sweetness" although one may have tasted *sweet things;* no one ever saw "red," although one may have seen *red things;* no one ever saw, heard, tasted or felt "courage" in another, although one may have seen *courageous people.* Abstract ideas are merely the mental conception of *qualities* or *properties* divorced from their associated objects by Abstraction.

Conception or Generalization is that faculty of the Mind by which it forms and groups together several particular ideas in the form of *a general idea.* By the processes of Conception we form *classes* or *generalizations* from particular ideas arising from our *percepts.* First, we *perceive* things; then we *compare* them with each other; then we abstract their particular qualities, which are not common to the several objects; then we *generalize* them according to their resemblances; then we *name* the generalized concept. From these combined processes we form a Concept, or *general idea* of the class of things to which the particular things belong. Thus from subjecting a number of cows to this process, we arrive at the general Concept of "Cow." This general Concept includes all the qualities and properties *common to all cows*, while omitting those which are not common to the class. Or, we may form a concept of Napoleon Bonaparte, by combining his several qualities and properties and thus form a *general idea* of the man.

Judgment is that faculty of the Mind whereby we determine the agreement or disagreement between two concepts, ideas, or objects of thought, by comparing them with each other. From this comparison arises the judgment, which is expressed in the shape of a logical *proposition:* "The horse is an animal;" or "the horse is not a cow." Judgment is also used in forming a concept, in the first place, for we must *compare qualities* before we can form a *general idea.*

Reasoning is that faculty of the Mind whereby we compare two Judgments, one with the other, and from the comparison deduce a third Judgment. This is a form of indirect or mediate comparison, whereas the Judgment is a form of immediate or direct comparison. From this process of Reasoning arises a result which is expressed in what is called a Syllogism, as for instance: "All dogs are animals; Carlo is a dog; therefore, Carlo is an animal." Or expressed in symbols: "A equals C; and B equals C;" therefore, "A equals B." Reasoning is of two kinds or classes; *viz.*, Inductive and Deductive, respectively. We have explained these forms of Reasoning in detail in another volume of this series.

The Feelings are the mental faculties whereby we experience emotions or feelings. Feelings are the experiencing of the agreeable or disagreeable nature of our mental states. They can be defined only in their own terms. If we have never experienced a feeling, we cannot understand the words expressing it. Feelings result in what are called emotion, affection and desire. An emotion is the simple feeling, such as joy, sorrow, etc. An affection is an emotion reaching out toward another and outside object, such as envy, jealousy, love, etc. A desire is an emotion arising from the *want* of some lacking quality or thing, and the inclination to possess it.

Memory is the faculty of the Mind whereby we retain and reproduce, or consciously revive any kind of past mental experience. It has two sub-phases; *viz.*, Retention and Recollection, respectively. It manifests in the storing away of mental images and ideas, and in the reproduction of them at a later period of time, and also of the recognition of them as objects of past experience.

Imagination is the faculty of the Mind whereby we represent (*re-pre-sent*) as a mental image some previously experienced idea, concept or image. Its activities are closely allied and blended with those of the Memory. It has the power not only of reproducing objects already perceived but also another power of *ideal creation* whereby it *creates* new combinations from the materials of past experience. It is a faculty, the importance of which is but little understood by the majority of men. Inasmuch as the mental image must always precede the material manifestation, the cultivation of the Imagination becomes a matter of great importance and worthy of the closest study.

Intuition is the faculty of the Mind whereby it evolves what have been called Primary Truths or Primary Ideas. By Primary Ideas are meant the ideas of Space, Time, Cause, Identity, etc. By Primary Truths are meant the so-called "Self-Evident Truths" of geometry, mathematics and logic. Under the head of Intuition are also sometimes included the activities of the Subconscious or Superconscious regions of the mind, of which we have spoken in detail in a volume under that name of this series. Some authorities hold to the older idea of "Innate Ideas" by which is meant that every human being is born with the knowledge of certain fundamental truths, unconnected with any experience. Others hold that these ideas are simply the result of the experience of the race, transmitted to us as "germ ideas" which must grow by experience and exercise.

That each and every faculty of the Mind may be strengthened and developed by Culture and Exercise is now held to be a fact by nearly every authority worthy of that name. Just as the physical muscle may be cultivated by the proper methods, so may the mental faculties be strengthened and cultivated by the appropriate methods and means. Inasmuch as the majority of the race are deficient in the development of one or more of the leading mental faculties, it becomes a matter of great interest and importance that all should acquaint themselves with the means whereby their deficiencies may be corrected and remedied. We shall now proceed to the consideration of Thought-Culture in general, and then to the consideration of the culture of each particular general faculty, in detail.

CHAPTER IV.

THOUGHT-CULTURE

Thought-Culture is based upon two general scientific facts which may be stated as follows:

I. The brain centres of thought may be developed by exercise. While we do not assert that the brain and the mind are identical, it is nevertheless a scientific truth that "the brain is the organ of the mind" and that one of the first requisites for a good mind is a good brain. It has been proven by experiment that the brain-cells concerned in special mental activities multiply in proportion to the active use of the special faculties employed in the mental operation. It has also been ascertained that disuse of special faculties of the mind tends to cause a process akin to atrophy in the brain-cells concerned in the particular activity, so that it becomes difficult to think clearly along those particular lines after a long period of disuse. Moreover, it is known that the education and mental culture of a child is accompanied by an increase and development of the brain-cells connected with the particular fields of thought in which the child is exercised.

There is a close analogy between the exercise of the brain-cells and the exercise of the muscles of the body. Both respond to reasonable exercise; both are injured by overwork; both degenerate by disuse. As Brooks says: "The mind grows by its own inherent energies. Mental exercise is thus the law of mental development. As a muscle grows strong by use, so any faculty of the mind is developed by its proper use and exercise. An inactive mind, like an unused muscle, becomes weak and unskilful. Hang the arm in a sling and the muscle becomes flabby and loses its vigor and skill; let the mind remain inactive and it acquires a mental flabbiness that unfits it for any severe or prolonged activity. An idle mind loses its tone and strength like an unused muscle; the mental powers go to rust through idleness and inaction. To develop the faculties of the mind and secure their highest activity and efficiency, there must be a constant and judicious exercise of these faculties. The object of culture is to stimulate and direct the activity of the mind."

Experiments conducted by scientists upon dogs have shown that in the case of dogs specially trained to unusual mental activity, there has been a corresponding increase of the number of active brain-cells in the particular parts of the brain concerned with those mental activities. Microscopic examination of the brain tissues showed the greatest difference between the brain structure of the trained dogs and untrained ones of the same brood. So carefully were the experiments conducted that it was possible to distinguish between the dogs trained in one set of activities from those trained in another. Biologists have demonstrated the correctness of the brain-cell development theory beyond reasonable doubt, and ordinary human experience also adds its testimony in its favor.

In view of the above, it will be seen that by intelligent exercise and use any and all faculties of the mind may be developed and cultivated, just as may any special muscle of the body. And this exercise can come only from actual use of the faculties themselves. Development must come from within and not from without. No system of outward stimulation will develop the faculties of the mind—they may be cultivated only by an exercise in their own particular field of work. The only way to exercise any particular faculty of thought is to *think* through that faculty.

II. Not only are the brain-cells developed by exercise, but it also appears to be a fact that the mind appears actually to be *nourished* by knowledge of the outside world of things. The raw material of thought is taken into the mind and there is digested by the thought-processes, and is afterward actually *assimilated* by the mind in a manner strikingly similar to the processes of the physical organs of nutrition. A mind to be at its best must be supplied with a normal amount of mental nourishment. Lacking this, it tends to become weak and inefficient. And, likewise, if its owner is a mental glutton and furnishes too much nourishment, particularly of a rich kind, there is a tendency toward "mental dyspepsia" and indigestion—the mind, unable to assimilate the mental food furnished it, is inclined to rebel. Moreover, if the mind be supplied with mental food of only one kind—if the mind is confined to one narrow field of thought

—it weakens and the mental processes become impaired. In many ways is this curious analogy apparent.

Not only does the mind need development, but it also needs intelligent cultivation. For it may be *developed* by improper objects of thought just as well as by the proper ones. A rich field will grow tares and weeds as well as good grain or fruit. Thought-culture should not be confined to the *development of a strong and active mind,* but should be also extended to the *cultivation of a wise and intelligent mind.* Strength and Wisdom should be combined. Moreover there should be sought a harmonious and normal development. A one-sided mental development is apt to produce a "crank," while a development in unhealthy mental fields will produce an abnormal thinker tending dangerously near to the line of insanity. Some "one-idea" men have great mental power and development, but are nevertheless unbalanced and impractical. And insane persons often have strongly developed minds—developed abnormally.

Some authorities, holding special theories regarding the nature of mind, hold that

Thought-Culture is merely a *training* of the faculties rather than a *creation* of new mental power, inasmuch as the mind cannot be built up from the outside. This is a curious combination of truth and error. It is true that the mind cannot be built up from outside material, in the sense of creating *new mind,* but it is also true that in every mind there is the potentiality of growth and development. Just as the future oak is said to be in the acorn, so are the potentialities of mind-growth in every mind waiting for nourishment from outside and the proper cultivation. Brooks has well stated this, as follows: "The culture of the mind is not creative in its character; its object is to develop existing possibilities into realities. The mind possesses innate powers which may be awakened into a natural activity. The design of culture is to aid nature in improving the powers she has given. No new power can be created by culture; we can increase the activity of these powers, but cannot develop any new activities. Through these activities new ideas and thoughts may be developed, and the sum of human knowledge increased; but this is accomplished by a high activity of the natural powers with which the mind is endowed, and not by the culture of new powers. The profound philosopher uses the same faculties that the little child is developing in the games of the nursery. The object of culture is to arouse the powers which nature has given us into a normal activity and to stimulate and guide them in their unfolding."

In connection with the objection above mentioned, it may be said that while the development of the mind must come from within itself, rather than from without, nevertheless, in order to develop, it must have the nourishing material from the outside world in order to grow. Just as the body can grow from within only by the aid of nourishment from outside, so the mind, while growing from within, needs the material for thought which can come only from without itself. Thought requires "things" upon which to exercise itself—and upon which it is nourished. Without these outside objects, it can have no exercise and can receive no nourishment. Thought consists in the perception, examination and comparison of *things*, and the consequent building up new combinations, arrangements and syntheses. Therefore, the perceptive faculties are most necessary to Thought, and their culture is most necessary in the general work of Thought-Culture.

It must not be lost sight of that in Thought-Culture there is necessary a variety of exercises and forms of nourishment. What will develop one faculty will exert but a faint effect upon others. Each needs its own particular kind of exercise—each its particular kind of mental nourishment. While it is true that there is a certain benefit gained by the entire mind from an exercise of any of its parts, this effect is but secondary in importance. A man well developed mentally has been developed in each faculty, each in its own way. The faculty of perception requires objects of perception; the faculty of imagination requires objects of imagination; the faculty of reasoning requires objects of reasoning; and so on, each requiring objects of exercise and nourishment of its own kind—in its own class. In some persons some of the faculties are well developed while others are deficient. It follows that in such a case the weak faculties should be developed first, that they be brought up to the general standard. Then a further general development may be undertaken if desired. Moreover, in general development, it will be found that certain faculties will respond more readily to the cultivation given, while others will be slow to respond. In such cases wisdom dictates that a greater degree of exercise and nourishment be given to the slower and less responsible faculties, while the more responsive be given but a lighter development. In Thought-Culture as in physical culture, the less developed and slower responding parts should be given special attention.

In the following chapters we shall point out the methods and exercises calculated to develop the several faculties of the mind to the best advantage, in each case giving general advice along the lines of the cultivation of the particular faculty which will serve as general instruction regarding its culture. The student should carefully study the entire work before he attempts to specialize in the development of any particular faculty. The particular work may be aided by an acquaintance with the entire field of Thought-Culture for many of the faculties shade into each other in their activities and are always more or less interdependent. For, be it remembered, the mind is a *whole*, and not a mere aggregation of many parts. To understand the parts, one must study the whole—to understand the whole, one must study the parts.

CHAPTER V.

ATTENTION

Attention is not a faculty of the mind in the same sense as perception, abstraction, judgment, etc., but is rather in the nature of an act of will concerned in the focusing of the consciousness upon some object of thought presented or represented to the mind. In some respects it bears a resemblance to Abstraction, inasmuch as it sets aside some particular object for the consideration of the consciousness, to the exclusion of other objects. Wayland explains attention as a condition of mind in which the consciousness is excited and directed by an act of the will. Hamilton says: "Consciousness may be compared to a telescope; Attention is the pulling out and pressing in of the tubes in accommodating the focus of the eye;" and also that: "An act of attention, that is an act of concentration, seems thus necessary to every exertion of consciousness, as a certain contraction of the pupil is requisite to every exertion of vision. . . .

Attention then is to consciousness what the contraction of the pupil is to sight, or to the eye of the mind what the microscope or telescope is to the bodily eye. . . . It constitutes the better half of all intellectual power."

Brodie says that: "It is Attention, much more than any difference in the abstract power of reasoning, which constitutes the vast difference which exists between minds of different individuals." Butler says: "The most important intellectual habit that I know of is the habit of attending exclusively to the matter in hand. . . . It is commonly said that genius cannot be infused by education, yet this power of concentrated attention, which belongs as a part of his gift to every great discoverer, is unquestionably capable of almost indefinite augmentation by resolute practice." And Beattie says: "The force wherewith anything strikes the mind is generally in proportion to the degree of attention bestowed upon it."

Realizing the importance of attention, the student will naturally wish to cultivate the power of bestowing it when necessary. The first role in the cultivation of the attention is that the student shall carefully acquire *the habit of thinking of or doing but one thing at a time.* This first rule may seem easy, but in practice it will be found very difficult of observance, so careless are the majority of us in our actions and thinking. Not only will the trouble and care bestowed upon the acquiring of this habit of thought and action be well repaid by the development of the attention, but the student will also acquire a facility for accomplishing his tasks quickly and thoroughly. As Kay says: "There is nothing that contributes more to success in any pursuit than that of having the attention concentrated on the matter in hand; and, on the contrary, nothing is more detrimental than when doing one thing to have the mind taken up with something else." And as Granville says: "A frequent cause of failure in the faculty of attention is striving to think of more than one thing at a time." Kay also well says: "If we would possess the power of attention in a high degree, we must cultivate the habit of attending to what is directly before the mind, to the exclusion of all else. All distracting thoughts and feelings that tend to withdraw the mind from what is immediately before it are therefore to be carefully avoided. This is a matter of great importance, and of no little difficulty. Frequently the mind, in place of being concentrated on what is immediately before it, is thinking of something else—something, it may be, that went before or that may come after, or something quite alien to the subject.''

The following principles of the application of the attention have been stated by the authorities:

I. The attention attaches more readily to interesting than to uninteresting things.

II. The attention will decline in strength unless there is a variation in the stimulus, either by a change of object or the developing of some new attribute in the object.

III. The attention, when tired by continuous direction toward some unvarying object, may be revived by directing it toward some new object or in allowing it to be attracted and held by some passing object.

IV. The attention manifests in a two-fold activity; *viz.* (1) the concentration upon some one object of thought; and (2) the shutting out of outside objects. Thus, it has its positive and negative sides. Thus, when a man wishes to give his undivided attention to one speaker in a crowd of speaking individuals, he acts positively in focusing his consciousness upon the selected individual, and negatively by refusing to listen to the others.

V. The attention is not a faculty, but a means of using any faculty with an increased degree of efficiency.

VI. The degree of attention possessed by an individual is an indication of his power of using his intellect. Many authorities have held that, in cases of genius, the power of concentrated attention is usually greatly developed. Brooks says: "Attention is one of the principal elements of genius." Hamilton says: "Genius is a higher capacity of attention." Helvetius says: "Genius is nothing but protracted attention." Chesterfield says: "The power of applying our attention, steady and undissipated, to a single object is a sure mark of superior genius."

The attention may be cultivated, just as may be the various faculties of the mind, by the two-fold method of Exercise and Nourishment; that is, by using and employing it actively and by furnishing it with the proper materials with which to feed its strength. The way to exercise the attention is *to use it frequently* in every-day life. If you are listening to a man speaking, endeavor to give to him your undivided attention, and, at the same time, to shut out from your consciousness every other object. In working, we should endeavor to use the attention by concentrating our interest upon the particular task before us to the exclusion of all else. In reading, we should endeavor to hold our minds closely to the text instead of hastily glancing over the page as so many do.

Those who wish to cultivate their attention should take up some line of study in which it is necessary to fasten the attention firmly for a time. A half-hour's study in this way is worth more than hours of careless reading so far as the cultivation of the attention is concerned. Mathematics is most valuable in the direction of developing the power of attention. Gibbon says: "After a rapid glance on the subject and distribution of a new book, I suspend the reading of it which I only resume after having myself examined the subject in all its relations."

Some writers have held that the attention may be developed by the practice of selecting the voice of one person speaking among a crowd of speakers, and deliberately shutting out the other sounds, giving the whole attention to the particular speaker; or, in the same manner, selecting one singer in a church choir or band of singers; or one musical instrument in an orchestra; or one piece of machinery making sounds in a room filled with various machines, etc. The practice of so doing is held to strengthen one's powers of concentration and attention.

Draper says: "Although many images may be simultaneously existing upon the retina, the mind possesses the power of singling out any one of them and fastening attention upon it, just as among a number of musical instruments simultaneously played, one, and that perhaps the feeblest, may be selected and its notes exclusively followed." And as Taylor says: "In a concert of several voices, the voices being of nearly equal intensity, regarded merely as organic impressions on the auditory nerve, we select one, and at will we lift out and disjoin it from the general volume of sound; we shut off the other voices—five, ten and more—and follow this one alone. When we have done so for a time, we freely cast it off and take up another." Carpenter says: "The more completely the mental energy can be brought into one focus and all distracting objects excluded, the more powerful will be the volitional effort."

Many authorities hold that the attention may be best applied and exercised by analyzing an object mentally, and then considering its parts one by one by a process of abstraction. Thus, as Kays says: "An apple presents to us form, color, taste, smell, etc., and if we would obtain a clear idea of any one of these, we must contemplate it by itself and compare it with other impressions of the same kind we have previously experienced. So in viewing a landscape, it is not enough to regard it merely as a whole, but we must regard each of its different parts individually by itself if we would obtain a clear idea of it. We can only obtain a full and complete knowledge of an object *by analyzing it and concentrating the attention upon its different parts, one by one.*" Reid says: "It is not by the senses immediately, but rather by the power of *analyzing and abstraction,* that we get the most simple and the most distinct notions of objects of sense." And, as Brown says: "It is scarcely possible to advance even a single step in intellectual physics without the necessity of performing *some sort of analysis.*" In all processes requiring analysis and examination of parts, properties or qualities, the attention is actively employed. Accordingly, it follows that such exercises are best adapted to the work of developing and cultivating the attention itself. Therefore, as a parting word we may say: *To develop and cultivate the power of attention and concentration, (1) Analyze; (2) Analyze; and (3) Analyze. Analyze everything and everybody with which or whom you come in contact.* There is no better or shorter rule.

The student will also find that the various directions and the advice which we shall give in the succeeding chapters, regarding the cultivation of the various faculties, are also adapted to the development of the attention, for the latter is brought into active play in them. And, likewise, by developing the attention, one may practice the future exercises with greater effect.

CHAPTER VI.

PERCEPTION

In preceding chapters we have seen that in the phase of mental activity in which the Intellect is concerned, the processes of which are known as "Thought" in the narrower sense of the term, there are several stages or steps involving the use of several faculties of the mind. The first of these steps or stages is called *Perception.*

Many persons confuse the idea of Sensation and Perception, but there is a clear distinction between them. Sensations arise from nerve action—from the stimulation of nerve substance—which gives rise to a peculiar effect upon the brain, which results in an elementary form of consciousness. An authority says: "Sensation is the peculiar property of the nervous system in a state of activity, by which impressions are conveyed to the brain or sensorium. When an impression is made upon any portion of the bodily surface by contact, heat, electricity, light, or any other agent, the mind is rendered conscious of this by sensation. In the process there are three stages—reception of the impression at the end of the sensory nerve, the conduction of it along the nerve trunk to the sensorium, and *the change it excites in the sensorium itself, through which is produced sensation.*

Just why and how this nerve action is translated into consciousness of an elementary kind, science is unable to explain. Our knowledge is based in a great part, or entirely, upon impressions which have been received over the channel of the senses—sensations of sight, hearing, tasting, smelling and touch. Many authorities hold that all of the five senses are modifications of the sense of touch, or feeling; as for instance, the impression upon the organs of sight is really in the nature of a delicate touch or feeling of the light-waves as they come in contact with the nerves of vision, etc. But, although sensations give us the raw materials of thought, so to speak, they are not *knowledge* in themselves. Knowledge arises from the operation of Perception upon this raw material of Sensation.

But yet, Sensation plays a most active part

in the presentation of the raw material for the Perceptive faculties, and must not be regarded as merely a physiological process. It may be said to be the connecting link between the physical and the mental activities. As Ziehen says: "It follows that the constitution of the nervous system is an essential factor in determining the quality of sensation. This fact reveals the obvious error of former centuries, first refuted by Locke, though still shared by naive thought today, that the objects about us themselves are colored, warm, cold, etc. As external to our consciousness, we can only assume matter, vibrating with molecular motion and permeated by vibrating particles of ether. The nervous apparatus selects only certain motions of matter or of ether, which they transform into that form of nerve excitation with which they are familiar. It is only this nerve excitation that we perceive as red, warm or hard."

Passing from Sensation to Perception, we see that the latter interprets the reports of the former. Perception translates into consciousness the impressions of Sensation. Perception, acting through one or more of the mental faculties, gives us *our first bit of real knowledge.* Sensation may give us the impression of a small moving thing—Perception translates this into the thought of *a cat.* Sensation is a mere *feeling*—Perception is the *thought* arising from that feeling. A Percept is the product of Perception, or in other words, our *idea* gained through Perception. The majority of our percepts are complex, being built up from a number of minor percepts; as for instance, our percept of *a peach* is built up from our minor percepts of the form, shape, color, weight, degree of hardness, smell, taste, etc., of the peach, each sense employed giving minor percepts, the whole being combined in the conscious as the whole percept of that particular peach.

Brooks says: "All knowledge does not come directly from perception through the senses, however. We have a knowledge of external objects, and we have a knowledge that transcends this knowledge of external objects. Perception is the *immediate* source of the first kind of knowledge, and the *indirect* source of the second kind of knowledge. This distinction is often expressed by the terms *cause* and *occasion*. Thus perception is said to be the *cause* of our knowledge of objects, since it is the immediate source of such knowledge. Perception is also said to be the *occasion* of the ideas and truths of intuition; for, though in a sense necessary to these ideas, it is not the source of them. Perception also furnishes the understanding with materials out of which it derives ideas and truths beyond the field of sense. As thus attaining a knowledge of external objects, affording material for the operations of the understanding, and furnishing the occasion for the activity of the intuitive power, *perception may be said to lie at the basis of all knowledge.*"

Perception is of course manifest in all persons. But it varies greatly in degree and power. Moreover, it may be developed and cultivated to a great degree. As Perception is an interpretation of the impression of the senses, we often confuse the cultivation of Perception with the development of the senses themselves. Two persons of equally perfect sense of sight may vary greatly in their degree of Perception of sight impressions. One may be a most careless observer, while the other may be a very close observer and able to distinguish many points of interest and importance in the object viewed which are not apparent to the first observer. Cultivation of Perception is cultivation of the *mental background of the senses*, rather than of the sense organs themselves. The Perception accompanying each sense may be developed and cultivated separately from that accompanying the others.

The majority of persons are very careless observers. They will *see* things without *perceiving* the qualities, properties, characteristics, or parts which together make up those things. Two persons, possessed of equal degrees of eyesight, will walk through a forest. Both of them will *see* trees. To one of them there will be but trees perceived; while to the other there will be a perception of the different species of trees, with their varying bark, leaves, shape, etc. One perceives simply a "pile of stone," which to the perception of another will be recognized as granite, marble, etc. Brooks says: "Very few persons can tell the difference between the number of legs of a fly and of a spider; and I have known farmers' boys and girls who could not tell whether the ears of a cow are in front of her horns, above her horns, below her horns, or behind her horns." Halleck says of a test in a schoolroom: "Fifteen pupils were sure that they had seen cats climb trees and descend them. There was a unanimity of opinion that the cats went up head first. When asked whether the cats came down head or tail first, the majority were sure that the cats descended as they were never known to do. Anyone who had ever noticed the shape of the claws of any beast of prey could have answered that question without seeing an actual descent. Farmers' boys, who have often seen cows and horses lie down and rise, are seldom sure whether the animals rise with their fore or hind feet first, or whether the habit of the horse agrees with that of the cow in this respect."

Brooks well says: "Modern education tends to the neglect of the culture of the perceptive powers. In ancient times people studied nature much more than at present. Being without books, they were compelled to depend upon their eyes and ears for knowledge; and this made their senses active, searching and exact. At the present day, we study books for a knowledge of external things; and we study them too much or too exclusively, and thus neglect the cultivation of the senses. We get our knowledge of the material world second-hand, instead of fresh from the open pages of the book of nature. Is it not a great mistake to spend so much time in school and yet not know the difference between the leaf of a beech and of an oak; or not be able to distinguish between specimens of marble, quartz, and granite? The neglect of the culture of the perceptive powers is shown by the scholars of the present time. Very few educated men are good observers; indeed, the most of them are sadly deficient in this respect. . . . They were taught to think and remember; but were not taught to use their eyes and ears. In modern education, books are used too much like spectacles, and the result is the blunting of the natural powers of perception."

The first principle in the Cultivation of Perception is the correct use of the Attention. The intelligent control of voluntary attention is a prerequisite to clear and distinct perception. We have called your attention to this matter in the preceding chapter. Halleck says: "A body may be imaged on the retina without insuring perception. There must be an effort to concentrate the attention upon the many things which the world presents to our senses. . . . Perception, to achieve satisfactory results, must summon the will to its aid to concentrate the attention. Only the smallest part of what falls upon our senses at any time is actually perceived."

The sense of sight is perhaps the one of the greatest importance to us, and accordingly the cultivation of Perception with regard to impressions received through the eye is the most important for the ordinary individual. As Kay says: "To see clearly is a valuable aid even to thinking clearly. In all our mental operations we owe much to sight. To recollect, to think, to imagine, is to see internally,—to call up more or less visual images of things before the mind. In order to understand a thing it is generally necessary to see it, and what a man has not seen he cannot properly realize or image distinctly to his mind. . . . It is by the habitual direction of our attention to the effects produced upon our consciousness by the impressions made upon the eye and transmitted to the sensorium that our sight, like our other senses, is trained." Bain says: "Cohering trains and aggregates of the sensations of sight make more than any other thing, perhaps more than all other things put together, the material of thought, memory and imagination." Vinet says: "The child, and perhaps the man as well, only knows well what is shown him, and the image of things is the true medium between their abstract idea and his personal experience." This being the case, advice concerning the Cultivation of Perception must needs be directed mainly to the cultivation of the perception of sight-impressions.

Brooks says: "We should acquire the habit of observing with attention. Many persons look at objects with a careless, inattentive eye. We should guard against the habit of careless looking. We should fix the mind upon the object before us; we should concentrate the attention upon that upon which we are looking. Attention, in respect to Perception, has been compared to a burning glass;

hold the sun-glass between the sun and a board and the concentrated rays will burn a hole through the latter. So attention concentrates the rays of perceptive power and enables the mind to penetrate below the surface of things."

The best authorities agree in the idea that the Perception may be best cultivated by acquiring the habit of examining things in detail. And, that this examination in detail is best manifested by examining the parts going to make up a complex thing, separately, rather than examining the thing as a whole. Halleck says regarding this point: "To look at things intelligently is the most difficult of all arts. The first rule for the cultivation of accurate perception is: Do not try to perceive the whole of a complex object at once. Take the human face for example. A man holding an important position to which he had been elected offended many people because he could not remember faces, and hence failed to recognize individuals the second time he met them. His trouble was in looking at the countenance as a whole. When he changed his method of observation, and noticed carefully the nose, mouth, eyes, chin and color of hair, he at once began to find recognition easier. He was no longer in danger of mistaking A for B, since he remembered that the shape of B's nose was different, or the color of his hair at least three shades lighter. This example shows that another rule can be formulated: Pay careful attention to details. . . . To see an object merely as an undiscriminated mass of something in a certain place is to do no more than a donkey accomplishes as he trots along."

Brooks says regarding the same point: "To train the powers of observation we should practice observing minutely. We should analyze the objects which we look at into their parts, and notice these parts. Objects present themselves to us as wholes; our definite knowledge of them is gained by analysis, by separating them into the elements which compose them. We should therefore give attention to the details of whatever we are considering; and thus cultivate the habit of observing with minuteness. . . . It is related of a teacher that if, when hearing a class, some one rapped at the door, he would look up as the visitor entered and from a single glance could tell his appearance and dress, the kind of hat he wore, kind of necktie, collar, vest, coat, shoes, etc. The skillful banker, also, in counting money with wondrous rapidity, will detect and throw from his pile of bills the counterfeits which, to the ordinary eye, seem to be without spot or blemish."

One of the best methods of developing and cultivating the faculty of Perception is to take up some study in which the perceptive faculties *must be* employed. Botany, physics, geology, natural history give splendid exercise in Perception, providing the student engages in actual experimental work, and actual observation, instead of confining himself to the text-books. A careful scientific study and examination of *any kind of objects*, in a manner calculated to bring out the various points of resemblance and difference, will do most to develop the Perception. Training of this kind will develop these powers to a high degree, in the case of small children.

Drawing is also a great help to the development of Perception. In order to draw a thing correctly we must of necessity examine it in detail; otherwise we will not be able to draw it correctly. In fact, many authorities use the test of drawing to prove the degree of attention and Perception that the student has bestowed upon an object which he has been studying. Others place an object before the pupil for a few minutes, and then withdraw it, the pupil then being required to draw the object roughly but with attention to its leading peculiarities and features. Then the object is again placed before the pupil for study, and he is then again required to draw from memory the additional details he has noticed in it. This process is repeated over and over again, until the pupil has proved that he has *observed* every possible detail of interest in the object. This exercise has resulted in the cultivation of a high degree of perception in many students, and its simplicity should not detract from its importance. Any person may practice this exercise by himself; or, better still, two or more students may combine and endeavor to excel each other in friendly rivalry, each endeavoring to discover the greatest number of details in the object considered. So rapidly do students improve under this exercise, that a daily record will show a steady advance. Simple exercises in drawing are found in the reproduction, from memory, of geography maps, leaves of trees, etc.

Similar exercises may be found in the practice of taking a hasty look at a person, animal or building, and then endeavoring to reproduce in writing the particular points about the person or thing observed. This exercise will reveal rapid progress if persisted in. Or, it may be varied by endeavoring to write out the contents of a room through which one has walked.

The majority of our readers remember the familiar story of Houdin, who so cultivated the faculty of Perception that he was able to pass by a shop-window and afterward state in detail every object in the window. He acquired this power by gradual development, beginning with the observation of a single article in the window, then two, then three and so on. Others have followed his method with great success. Speaking of Houdin's wonderful Perception, Halleck says: "A wide-awake eagle would probably see more of a thing at one glance than would a drowsy lizard in a quarter of an hour. Extreme rapidity of Perception, due to careful training, was one of the factors enabling Houdin and his son to astonish everybody and to amass a fortune. He placed a domino before the boy, and instead of allowing him to count the spots, required him to give the sum total at once. This exercise was continued until each could give instantaneously the sum of the spots on a dozen dominoes. The sum was given just as accurately as if five minutes had been consumed in adding." Houdin, in his Memoirs relating the above facts regarding his own methods, states with due modesty, that many women far excel him in this respect. He says: "I can safely assert that a lady seeing another pass at full speed in a carriage will have had time to analyze her toilette from her bonnet to her shoes, and be able to describe not only the fashion and quality of the stuffs, but also say if the lace be real or only machine made."

There are a number of games played by children which tend to the cultivation of the Perception, and which might well be adapted for the use of older people. These games are based on the general principle of the various participants taking a brief view of a number of objects displayed in one's hand, on a table, in a box, etc., and then stating what he or she has seen. There will be noticed a wonderful difference in the degree of Perception manifested by the various participants. And, equally interesting will be the degrees of progress noted after playing this game over several times, allowing time for rest between the series of games. It is a fact well known in police circles that thieves often train boys in this way, following this course by another in which the lads are expected to take in the contents of a room, the windows, locks, etc., at a glance. They are then graduated into spies looking out the details of the scenes of future robberies.

In our volume of this series, devoted to the consideration of the Memory, we have related a number of exercises and methods, similar to those given above, by which the Perception may be cultivated. Perception plays a most important place in memory, for upon the clearness of the percepts depends to a great degree the clearness of the impressions made upon the memory. So close is the connection between Memory and Perception that the cultivation of one tends to develop the other. For instance, the cultivation of the Memory necessitates the sharpening of the Perception in the direction of obtaining clear original impressions; while the cultivation of Perception naturally develops the Memory by reason of the fact that the latter is used in testing and proving the clearness and degree of Perception. This being the case, those who find that the exercises and methods given above are too arduous may substitute the simple exercise of remembering as many details as possible of things they see. This effort to impress the memory will involuntarily bring into action the perceptive faculties in the acquirement of the original impressions, so that in the end the Perception will be found to have developed.

Teachers and those having to do with children should realize the great value of the cultivation of Perception in the young, and thus establishing valuable habits of observation among them. The experience and culture thus acquired will prove of great value in their after life. As Brooks well says on this subject: "Teachers should appreciate the value of the culture of the perceptive powers, and endeavor to do something to afford this culture. Let it be remembered that by training the powers of observation of pupils, we lead them to acquire definite ideas of things, enable them to store their minds with fresh and interesting knowledge, lay the foundation for literary or business success, and thus do much to enhance their happiness in life and add to the sum of human knowledge."

CHAPTER VII.

REPRESENTATION

Sensation and Perception, as considered in the preceding chapter, are what are called by psychologists "Processes of Presentation." By Presentation is meant the direct offering to the consciousness of mental images or objects of thought. If there were no faculty of the mind capable of retaining and *re*-presenting to the consciousness the impression or record of Perception, we could never progress in knowledge, for each percept would be new each time it was presented and there would be no recognition of it as having been previously perceived, nor would there be any power to voluntarily recall any percept previously acquired. In short, we would be without that power of the mind called Memory.

But, fortunately for us as thinkers, we possess the power of Representation; that is, of reproducing past perceptions and experiences in the shape of *mental images* or pictures, "in the mind's eye," so to speak, which relieves us of the necessity of directly and immediately perceiving an object each time we desire or are required to think of it. The processes whereby this becomes possible are called the processes of Representation, for the reason that by them past experiences of Perception are *re*-presented to the consciousness.

The subject of Representation is closely bound up with that of Memory. Strictly speaking, Representation may be said to be one phase of Memory; Association of Ideas another; and the authorities prefer to treat the whole subject under the general head of Memory. We have written a work on "Memory" which forms one of the volumes of the present series, and we have no intention, or desire, to repeat here the information given in that work. But we must consider the subject of Representation at this point in order to maintain the logical unity of the present general subject of Thought-Culture. The student will also notice, of course, the close relation between the processes of Representation and those of the Imagination, which we shall consider in other chapters of this work.

Memory has several phases, the usual classification of which is as follows: (1) Impression; (2) Retention; (3) Recollection; (4) Representation, and (5) Recognition. Each phase requires the operation of special mental processes. *Impression* is the process whereby the impressions of Perception are recorded or stamped upon the subconscious field of mentality, as the impress of the die upon the wax. *Retention* is the process whereby the subconsciousness *retains* or holds the impressions so received. *Recollection* is the process by which the mind *re-collects* the impressions retained in the subconsciousness, bringing them again into consciousness as objects of knowledge. *Representation* is the process whereby the impressions so re-collected are *pictured or imaged* in the mind. *Recogniton* is the process whereby the mind *recognizes* the mental image or picture so re-presented to it as connected with its past experience.

As we have stated, we have considered the general subject of Memory in another volume of this series and, therefore, shall not attempt to enter into a discussion of its general subject at this place. We shall, accordingly, limit ourselves here to a brief consideration of the phase of Representation and its cultivation.

Representation, of course, depends upon the preceding phases of Memory known as Impression, Retention and Recollection. Unless the Impression is clear; unless the Retention is normal, there can be no Representation. And unless one *recollects* there can be no Representation. Recollection (which is really a re-collection of percepts) must precede Representation in the shape of mental images or pictures. Recollection re-collects the mental materials out of which the image is to be constructed. But, as Brooks says: "It is not to be assumed that knowledge is retained as a picture; but that it is *recreated* in the form of a picture or some other mental product when it is recalled." The process is analogous to the transmutation of the sound-waves entering the receiver of a telephone, into electrical-waves which are transmitted to the receiver, where they are in turn re-transmuted to sound-waves which enter the ear of the listener. It will be seen at once that there is the closest possible relation between the processes of Representation and those of Memory

—in fact, it is quite difficult to draw a clear line of division between them. Some make the distinction that Representation furnishes us with an exact reproduction of *the past*; while Imagination combines our mental images into *new products*. That is, Representation merely *reproduces*; while Imagination *creates* by forming new combinations; or Representation deals with a reproduction of the Actual; while Imagination deals with the Ideal.

Wundt speaking of this difficult distinction says: "Psychologists are accustomed to define *memory images* as ideas which *exactly reproduce* some previous perception, and *fancy images* as ideas consisting of a combination of elements taken from a whole number of perceptions. Now memory images in the sense of this definition simply do not exist. . . . Try, for instance, to draw from memory some landscape picture which you have only once seen, and then compare your copy with the original. You will expect to find plenty of mistakes and omissions; but you will also invariably find that you have put in a great deal which was not in the original, but which comes from landscape pictures which you have seen somewhere else.''

While we generally speak of Representation *picturing* the recollected percepts, still, we must not make the mistake of supposing that it is concerned with, or limited to, only mental pictures. We are able to *represent* not only visual percepts but also sounds, smells, tastes or feelings, often so vividly that they appear as almost actually existent. We may also even *represent*, symbolically the processes of reasoning, mathematical operations, etc. In short nearly, if not all experiences which are possible in Presentation are also possible in Representation.

The phase of Representation, in the processes of Memory, is of course subject to the general laws of the Cultivation of Memory which we have stated in detail in our previous volume on that subject. But there are some special points of development and cultivation which may be considered briefly in this place. In the first place the importance of Attention and clear Perception, as necessary precedents for clear Representation, may be emphasized. In order to form clear mental images of a thing we must have perceived it clearly in the first place. The advice regarding the use of the Attention and Perception given in preceding chapters need not be repeated here, but special attention should be directed toward them in connection with the processes of Representation. If we wish to cultivate the Representative faculties, we must begin by cultivating the Presentative faculties.

Then again we must remember what we have said elsewhere about the facts of development through (1) Use; and (2) Nourishment, in all mental faculties. We must begin to *use* the faculties of Representation in order to exercise them. We must give them *nourishment* in the shape of objects of mental food. That is to say we must furnish these faculties with *materials* with which they may grow and develop, and with exercise in order to strengthen the mental-muscle and also to give the faculties the opportunity to "acquire the knack." The exercises and methods recommended in our chapter on Perception will furnish good *material* for the Representative faculties' growing requirements. By *perceiving* the details of things, one is able to reproduce clear mental images of them. In studying an object, always carry in your mind the fact that you wish to *reproduce* it in your mind later. In fact, if you have the opportunity, let your mind "repeat it to itself" as soon as possible after the actual occurrence and experience. Just as you often murmur to yourself, or else write down, the name of a person or place which you have just heard, in order that you may recollect it the better thereafter, so it will be well for you to "mentally repeat" to yourself the experiences upon which you wish to exercise your Representative faculties.

As to the matter of development and cultivation by Use, we would advise that you begin gradually to train your mind to *reproduce* the experiences of the day or week or month, at intervals, until you feel that you are developing a new power in that direction. Tonight, if you try you will find that you can reproduce but a very small part of today's happenings with any degree of clearness. How clearly can you image the places you have been, the appearances of the people you have met, the various details of persons and things which you perceived during the experiences of the day? Not very clearly, we dare say. Try again, and you will find that you will be able to add new details. Keep it up until you feel tired or think that you have exhausted all the possibilities of the task. Tomorrow, try it again, and you will find that the second day's experiences are more clearly reproduced in your mind. Each day should find you a little more advanced, until you get to a place where the normal degree of power is attained, when the advance will be slower.

Then, at the end of the week, review its experiences. Do the same the following week. At the end of the month, take a hasty mental trip over the month's experiences. And so on. Exercise, in moderation, along these lines will work wonders for you. Not only will it develop the Representation, but your powers of observation and your general memory will be found to be improved. And, moreover, in "chewing the mental cud" you will think of many things of interest and importance in connection with your work, etc., and your general mental efficiency will be increased for the faculties of the mind are interdependent and share benefits with each other.

CHAPTER VIII.

ABSTRACTION

As we have seen, the first stage or step in the process of Thought is that called Perception, which we have considered in the preceding chapter. Perception, as we have seen, is the process by which we gain our first knowledge of the external world as reported to us by the channels of sense. The Perceptive faculties interpret the material which is presented to us by the senses. Following upon Perception we find the processes resulting from the exercise of the group of faculties which are classified under the general head of Understanding.

Understanding is the faculty, or faculties, of the mind by means of which we intelligently examine and compare the various *percepts*, either separating them by analysis, or else combining them by synthesis, or both, and thus securing our general ideas, principles, laws, classes, etc. There are several subphases of Understanding which are known to psychologists and logicians as: (1) Abstraction; (2) Conception or Generalization; (3) Judgment, and (4) Reasoning, respectively. In this chapter we shall consider the first of these sub-phases or steps of Understanding, which is known as "Abstraction."

Abstraction is that faculty of the mind by which we abstract or "draw off," and then consider apart, the particular qualities, properties, or attributes of an object, and thus are able to consider *them* as "things" or objects of thought. In order to form *concepts* or general ideas, from our *percepts* or particular ideas, we must consider and examine two common points or qualities which go to make up *differences and resemblances.* The special examination or consideration of these common points or qualities result in the exercise of Abstraction. In the process of Abstraction we mentally "draw away" a quality of an object and then consider it as a distinct object of thought. Thus in considering a flower we may *abstract* its qualities of fragrance, color, shape, etc., and think of these as things independent of the flower itself from which they were derived. We think of *redness, fragrance,* etc., not only in connection with the particular flower but as *general qualities.* Thus the qualities of redness, sweetness, hardness, softness, etc., lead us to the abstract terms, *red, sweet, hard, soft, etc.* In the same way courage, cowardice, virtue, vice, love, hate, etc., are abstract terms. No one ever saw one of these things—they are known only in connection with objects, or else as "abstract terms" in the processes of Thought. They may be known as qualities, and expressed as predicates; or they may be considered as abstract things and expressed as nouns.

In the general process of Abstraction we first draw off and set aside all the qualities which are *not common* to the general class under consideration, for the concept or general idea must comprise only the qualities common to its class. Thus in the case of the general idea of horse, size and color must be abstracted as non-essentials, for horses are of various colors and sizes. But on the other hand, there are certain qualities which *are common to all horses,* and these must be abstracted and used in making up the concept or general idea.

So, you see, in general Abstraction we form two classes: (1) the unlike and not-general qualities; and (2) the like or common qualities. As Halleck says: "In the process of Abstraction, we draw our attention away from a mass of confusing details, unimportant at the time, and attend only to qualities common to the class. Abstraction is little else than centering the power of attention on some qualities to the exclusion of others. . . . While we are forming concepts, we abstract or draw off certain qualities, either to leave them out of view or to consider them by themselves. Our dictionaries contain such words as purity, whiteness, sweetness, industry, courage, etc. No one ever touched, tasted, smelled, heard, or saw purity or courage. We do not, therefore, gain our knowledge of these through the senses. We have seen pure persons, pure snow, pure honey; we have breathed pure air, tasted pure coffee. From all these different objects we have abstracted the only like quality, the quality of being pure. We then say we have an idea of *purity*, and that idea is an abstract one. It exists only in the mind which formed it. No one ever saw *whiteness.* He may have seen white clouds, snow, cloth, blossoms, houses, paper, horses, but he never saw *whiteness* by itself. He simply abstracted that quality from various white objects."

In Abstraction we may either (1) abstract a quality and set it aside and apart from the other qualities under consideration, as being non-essential and not necessary; or we may (2) abstract a quality and hold it in the mind as essential and necessary for the concept which we are forming. Likewise, we may abstract (1) all the qualities of an object *except one,* and set them aside that we may consider the *one* quality by itself; or we may (2) abstract the one particular quality and consider it to the exclusion of all its associated qualities. In all of these aspects we have the same underlying process of considering a quality apart from its object, and apart from its associated qualities. The mind more commonly operates in the direction of abstracting one quality and viewing it apart from object and associated qualities.

The importance of correct powers of Abstraction is seen when we realize that all concepts or general ideas are but combinations of abstract qualities or ideas. As Halleck says: "The difference between an *abstract idea* and a *concept* is that a concept may consist of a bundle of abstract ideas. If the class contains more than one common quality, so must the concept; it must contain as many of these abstracted qualities as are common to the class. The concept of the class *whale* would embody a large number of such qualities." As Brooks says: "If we could not abstract, we could not *generalize*, for abstraction is a condition of generalization." The last-mentioned authority also cleverly states the idea as follows: "The products of Abstraction are *abstract ideas*, that is, ideas of qualities in the abstract. Such ideas are called *Abstracts*. Thus my idea of some particular color, or hardness, or softness, is an abstract. Abstract ideas have been wittily called 'the ghosts of departed qualities.' They may more appropriately be regarded as the spirits of which the objects from which they are derived are the bodies. In other words, they are, figuratively speaking, 'the disembodied spirits of material things.' "

The cultivation of the faculty of Abstraction depends very materially, in the first place, upon the exercise of Attention and Perception. Mill holds that Abstraction is primarily a result of Attention. Others hold that it is merely the mental process by which the attention is directed exclusively to the consideration of one of several qualities, properties, attributes, parts, etc. Hamilton says: "Attention and Abstraction then are only the same process viewed in different relations. They are, as it were, the positive and negative poles of the same act." The cultivation of Attention is really a part of the process of the cultivation of the faculty of Abstraction. Unless the Attention be directed toward the object and its qualities we will be unable to perceive, set aside, and separately consider the abstract quality contained within it. In this process, as indeed in all other mental processes, Attention is a prerequisite. Therefore, here, as in many other places, we say to you: "Begin by cultivating Attention."

Moreover, the cultivation of the faculty of Abstraction depends materially upon the cultivation of Perception. Not only must we *sense* the existence of the various qualities in an object, but we must also *perceive* them in consciousness, just as we perceive the object itself. In fact, the perception of the object is merely a perception of its various qualities, attributes and properties, for the object itself is merely a composite of these abstract things, at least so far as its perception in consciousness is concerned. Try to think of *a horse*, without considering its qualities, attributes and properties, and the result is merely *an abstract horse*—something which belongs to the realm of unreality. Try to think of *a rose* without considering its color, odor, shape, size, response to touch, etc., and you have simply *an ideal rose* which when analyzed is seen to be a *nothing*. Take away the qualities, properties and attributes of anything, and you have left *merely a name*, or else a transcendental, idealistic, something apart from our world of sense knowledge. Thus it follows that in order to *know* the qualities of a thing in order to classify it, or to form a general idea of it, we *must* use the Perception in order to interpret or translate the sense-impressions we have received regarding them. Consequently the greater our power of Perception the greater must be the possibility of our power of Abstraction.

Beyond the cultivation, use and exercise of the Attention and the Perception, there are but few practical methods for cultivating the faculty of Abstraction. Of course, *exercise* of the faculty will develop it; and *the furnishing of material for its activities* will give it the "nourishment" of which we have spoken elsewhere. Practice in distinguishing the various qualities, attributes and properties of objects will give a valuable training to the faculty.

Let the student take any object and endeavor to analyze it into its abstract qualities, etc. Let him try to discover qualities hidden from first sight. Let him make a list of these qualities, and write them down; then try to add to the list. Two or more students engaging in a friendly rivalry will stimulate the efforts of each other. In children the exercise may be treated as a game. *Analysis of objects into their component qualities, attributes and qualities—the effort to extract as many adjectives applicable to the object*—this is the first step. The second step consists in *trans-*

forming these adjectives into their corresponding nouns. As for instance, in a rose we perceive the *qualities* which we call "redness," "fragrance," etc. We speak of the rose as being "red" or "fragrant"—then we think of "redness," or "fragrance" as abstract qualities, or things, which we express as nouns. Exercise and practice along these lines will tend to cultivate the faculty of Abstraction. By knowing qualities, we know the things possessing them.

CHAPTER IX.

ASSOCIATION OF IDEAS

Having formed general ideas, or Concepts, it is important that we associate them with other general ideas. In order to fully *understand* a general idea we must know its associations and relations. The greater the known associations or relations of an idea, the greater is our degree of understanding of that idea. If we simply know many thousands of separated general ideas, without also knowing their associations and relations, we are in almost as difficult a position as if we merely knew thousands of individual percepts without being able to classify them in general concepts. It is necessary to develop the faculty of associating ideas into groups, according to their relations, just as we group particular ideas in classes. The difference, however, is that these group-ideas do not form classes of a genus, but depend solely upon associations of several kinds, as we shall see in a moment.

Halleck says: "All ideas have certain definite associations with other ideas, and they come up in groups. There is always an association between our ideas, although there are cases when we cannot trace it. . . . Even when we find no association between our ideas, we may be sure that it exists. . . . An idea, then, never appears in consciousness unless there is a definite reason why this idea should appear in preference to others." Brooks says: "One idea or feeling in the mind calls up some other idea or feeling with which it is in some way related. Our ideas seem, as it were, to be tied together by the invisible thread of association, so that as one comes out of unconsciousness, it draws another with it. Thoughts seem to exist somewhat in clusters like the grapes of a bunch, so that in bringing out one, we bring the entire cluster with it. The law of association is thus the tie, the thread, the golden link by which our thoughts are united in an act of reproduction."

The majority of writers confine their consideration of Association of Ideas to its relation to Memory. It is true that the Laws of Association play an important part in Memory Culture, but Association of Ideas also form an important part of the general subject of Thought-Culture, and especially in the phase of the latter devoted to the development of the Understanding. The best authorities agree upon this idea and state it positively. Ribot says: "The most fundamental law which regulates psychological phenomena is the Law of Association. In its comprehensive character it is comparable to the law of attraction in the physical world." Mill says: "That which the law of gravitation is to astronomy, that which the elementary properties of the tissues are to physiology, the Law of Association of Ideas is to psychology."

There are two general principles, or laws, operative in the processes of Association of Ideas, known as (1) Association by Contiguity; and (2) Association by Similarity, respectively.

Association by Contiguity manifests particularly in the processes of memory. In its two phases of (1) Contiguity of Time; and (2) Contiguity of Space, respectively, it brings together before the field of consciousness ideas associated with each by reason of their time or space relations. Thus, if we remember a certain thing, we find it easy to remember things which occurred immediately before, or immediately after that particular thing. Verbal memory depends largely upon the contiguity of time, as for instance, our ability to repeat a poem, or passage from a book, if we can recall the first words thereof. Children often possess this form of memory to a surprising degree; and adults with only a limited degree of understanding may repeat freely long extracts from speeches they have heard, or even arbitrary jumbles of words. Visual memory depends largely upon contiguity of space, as for instance our ability to recall the details of scenes, when starting from a given point. In both of these forms of association by contiguity the mental operation is akin to that of unwinding a ball of yarn, the ideas, thus associated in the sequence of time or place, following each other into the field of consciousness. Association by Contiguity, while important in itself, properly belongs to the general subject of Memory, and as we have considered it in the volume of this series devoted to the last mentioned subject, we shall not speak of it further here.

Association by Similarity, however, posses-ses a special interest to students of the partic-ular subject of the culture of the Understand-ing. If we were compelled to rely upon the association of contiguity for our understand-ing of things, we would understand a thing merely in its relations to that which went be-fore or came after it; or by the things which were near it in space—we would have to un-wind the mental ball of time and space relations in order to bring into consciousness the associated relations of anything. The Asso-ciation of Similarity, however, remedies this defect, and gives us a higher and broader asso-ciation. Speaking of Association of Similar-ity, Kay says: "It is of the utmost impor-tance to us in forming a judgment of things, or in determining upon a particular line of conduct, to be able to bring together before the mind a number of instances of a *similar* kind, recent or long past, which may aid us in coming to a right determination. Thus, we may judge of the nature or quality of an arti-cle, and obtain light and leading in regard to any subject that may be before us. In this way we arrange and classify and reason by induction. *This is known as rational or philosophical association.*"

Halleck says: "An eminent philosopher has said that man is completely at the mercy of the association of his ideas. Every new object is seen in the light of its associated ideas. . . . It is not the business of the psychologist to state what power the association of ideas *ought* to have. It is for him to ascertain what power it *does* have. When we think of the bigotry of past ages, of the stake for the martyr and the stoning of witches, we can realize the force of Prof. Ziehen's statement: 'We cannot think as we *will*, but we *must* think as just those associations which happen to be present prescribe.' While this is not literally true, it may serve to emphasize a deflecting factor which is usually underestimated."

Locke says: "The connection in our minds of ideas, in themselves loose and independent of one another, has such an influence, and is of so great force, to set us awry in our actions, as well moral as natural, passions, reasonings, and notions themselves, that, perhaps, there is not any one thing that deserves more to be looked after." Stewart says: "The bulk of mankind, being but little accustomed to reflect and to generalize, associate their ideas chiefly according to their more obvious relations, and above all to the casual relations arising from contiguity in time and place; whereas, in the mind of a philosopher ideas are commonly associated according to those relations which are brought to light in consequence of particular efforts of attention, such as the relations of cause and effect, or of premises and conclusion. Hence, it must necessarily happen that when he has occasion to apply to use his acquired knowledge, time and reflection will be requisite to enable him to recollect it."

This Association by Similarity, or the "rational and philosophical association of ideas," may be developed and cultivated by a little care and work. The first principle is that of *learning the true relations of an idea*—its various logical associations. Perhaps the easiest and best method is that adopted and practiced by Socrates, the old Greek philosopher, often called "the Socratic method"—the Method of Questioning. By questioning oneself, or others, regarding a thing, the mind of the person answering tends to unfold its stores of information, and to make new and true associations. Kays says: "Socrates, Plato, and others among the ancients and some moderns, have been masters of this art. The principle of asking questions and obtaining answers to them may be said to characterize all intellectual effort. . . . The great thing is to ask the right questions, and to obtain the right answers." Meiklejohn says: "This art of questioning possessed by Dr. Hodgson was something wonderful and unique, and was to the minds of most of his pupils a truly obstetric art. He told them little or nothing, but showed them how to find out for themselves. 'The Socratic method,' he said, 'is the true one, especially with the young.' "

But this questioning must be done logically, and orderly, and not in a haphazard way. As Fitch says: "In proposing questions it is very necessary to keep in view the importance of arranging them in the exact order in which the subject would naturally develop itself in the mind of a logical and systematic thinker." A number of systems have been formulated by different writers on the subject, all of which have much merit. The following System of Analysis, designed for the use of students desiring to acquire correct associations, was given in the volume of this series, entitled "Memory," and is reproduced here because it is peculiarly adapted to the cultivation and development of the faculty of discovering and forming correct associations and relations between ideas:

SYSTEM OF ANALYSIS

When you wish to discover what you really *know* regarding a thing, ask yourself the following questions about it, examining each point in detail, and endeavoring to bring before the mind *your full knowledge* regarding that particular point. Fill in the deficiencies by reading some good work of reference, an encyclopedia for instance; or consulting a good dictionary, or both:

I. Where did it come from, or originate?

II. What caused it?

III. What history or record has it?

IV. What are its attributes, qualities or characteristics?

V. What things can I most readily associate with it? What is it most like?

VI. What is it good for—how may it be used—what can I do with it?

VII. What does it prove—what can be deduced from it?

VIII. What are its natural results—what happens because of it?

IX. What is its future; and its natural or probable end or finish?

X. What do I think of it, on the whole—what are my general impressions regarding it?

XI. What do I know about it, in the way of general information?

XII. What have I heard about it, and from whom, and when?

The following "Query Table," from the same volume, may be found useful in the same direction. It is simpler and less complicated than the system given above. It has well been called a "Magic Key of Knowledge," and it opens many a mental door:

QUERY TABLE

Ask yourself the following questions regarding the thing under consideration. It will draw out many bits of information and associated knowledge in your mind:

I. What?	IV. When?
II. Whence?	V. How?
III. Where?	VI. Why?

VII. Whither?

Remember, always, that the greater the number of associated and related ideas that you are able to group around a concept, the richer, fuller and truer does that concept become to you. The concept is a *general idea*, and its attributes of "generality" depend upon the associated facts and ideas related to it. The greater the number of the view points from which a concept may be examined and considered, the greater is the degree of knowledge concerning that concept. It is held that everything in the universe is related to every other thing, so that if we knew *all* the associated ideas and facts concerning a thing, we would not only know that particular thing *absolutely*, but would, besides, know *everything* in the universe. The chain of Association is infinite in extent.

CHAPTER X.

GENERALIZATION

We have seen that Sensation is translated or interpreted into Perception; and that from the Percepts so created we may "draw off," or separate, various qualities, attributes and properties by the analytical process we call Abstraction. Abstraction, we have seen, thus constitutes the first step in the process of what is called Understanding. The second step is called Generalization or Conception.

Generalization, or Conception, is that faculty of the mind by which we are able to combine and group together several particular ideas into one general idea. Thus when we find a number of particular objects possessing the same general qualities, attributes or properties, we proceed to *classify* them by the process of Generalization. For instance, in a number of animals possessing certain general and common qualities we form a concept of a class comprising those particular animals. Thus in the concept of cow, we include *all cows*

—we know them to be cows because of their possession of certain general class qualities which we include in our concept of *cow.* The particular cows may vary greatly in size, color and general appearance, but they possess the common general qualities which we group together in our general concept of *cow.* Likewise by reason of certain common and general qualities we include in our concept of "Man," *all men,* black, white, brown, red or yellow, of all races and degrees of physical and mental development. From this generic concept we may make race concepts, dividing men into Indians, Caucasians, Malays, Negroes, Mongolians, etc. These concepts in turn may be divided into sub-races. These sub-divisions result from an analysis of the great concept. The great concept is built up by synthesis from the individuals, through the sub-divisions of minor concepts. Or, again, we may form a concept of "Napoleon Bonaparte" from the various qualities and characteristics which went to make up that celebrated man.

The product of Generalization or Conception is called a *Concept.* A Concept is expressed in a word, or words, called "A Term."

A Concept is more than a mere *word*—it is *a general idea.* And a Term is more than a mere word—it is *the expression of a general idea.*

A *Concept* is built up from the processes of Perception, Abstraction, Comparison and Generalization. We must first perceive; then analyze or abstract qualities; then compare qualities; then synthesize or classify according to the result of the comparison of qualities. By perceiving and comparing the qualities of various individual things, we notice their points of resemblance and difference—the points wherein they agree or disagree—wherein they are alike or unlike. Eliminating by abstraction the points in which they differ and are unlike; and, again by abstraction, retaining in consideration the points in which they resemble and are alike; we are able to group, arrange or classify these *"alike things"* into *a class-idea* large enough to embrace them all. This class-idea is what is known as a General Idea or a Concept. This Concept we give a general name, which is called a Term. In grammar our particular ideas arising from Percepts are usually denoted by proper nouns—our general ideas arising from Concepts are usually denoted by common nouns. Thus "John Smith" (particular; proper noun) and "Man" (general; common noun). Or "horse" (general; common), and "Dobbin" (particular; proper).

It will be seen readily that there must be lower and higher concepts. Every class contains within itself lower classes. And every class is, itself, but a lower class in a higher one. Thus the high concept of "animal" may be analyzed into "mammal," which in turn is found to contain "horse," which in turn may be sub-divided into special kinds of horses. The concept "plant" may be subdivided many times before the concept "rose" is obtained, and the latter is capable of subdivision into varieties and sub-varieties, until at last a particular flower is reached. Jevons says: "We classify things together whenever we observe that they are like each other in any respect and, therefore, think of them together. . . . In classifying a collection of objects, we do not merely put together into groups those which resemble each other, but we also divide each class into smaller ones in which the resemblance is more complete. Thus the class of *white substances* may be divided into those which are solid and those which are fluid, so that we get the two minor classes of solid-white, and fluid-white substances. It is desirable to have names by which to show that one class is contained in another and, accordingly, we call the class which is divided into two or more smaller ones, the *Genus;* and the smaller ones into which it is divided, the *Species.*"

Every Genus is a Species of the class next higher than itself; and every Species is a Genus of the classes lower than itself. Thus it would seem that the extension in either direction would be infinite. But, for the purposes of finite thought, the authorities teach that there must be a Highest Genus, which cannot be the Species of a higher class, and which is called the *Summum Genus.* The *Summum Genus* is expressed by terms such as the following: "Being;" "Existence;" "The Absolute;" "Something;" "Thing;" "The Ultimate Reality," or some similar term denoting the state of being *ultimate.* Likewise, at the lowest end of the scale we find what are called the Lowest Species, or *Infima Species.* The Infima Species are always *individuals.* Thus we have the *individual* at one end of the scale; and *The Absolute* at the other. Beyond these limits the mind of man cannot travel.

There has been much confusion in making classifications and some ingenious plans have been evolved for simplifying the process. That of Jevons is perhaps the simplest, when understood. This authority says: "All these difficulties are avoided in the *perfect logical method of dividing each Genus into two Species, and not more than two, so that one species possesses a particular quality, and the other does not.* Thus if I divide dwelling-houses into those which are made of brick and those which are not made of brick, I am perfectly safe and nobody can find fault with me. . . . Suppose, for instance, that I divide dwelling-houses as below:

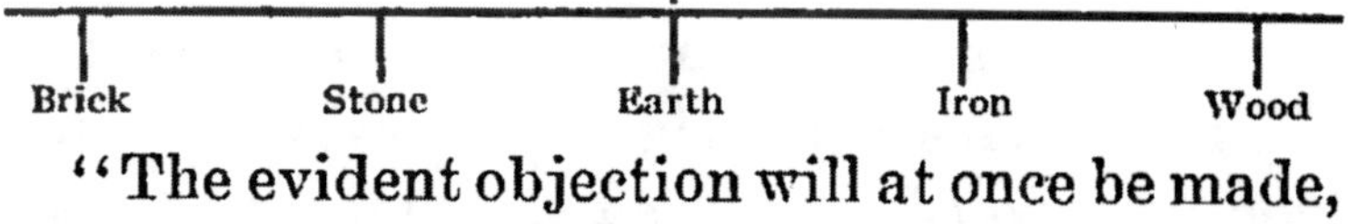

"The evident objection will at once be made, that houses may be built of other materials than those here specified. In Australia, houses are sometimes made of the bark of gum-trees; the Esquimaux live in snow houses; tents may be considered as canvas houses, and it is easy to conceive of houses made of terra-cotta, paper, straw, etc. All logical difficulties will, however, be avoided *if I never make more than two species at each step,* in the following way:—

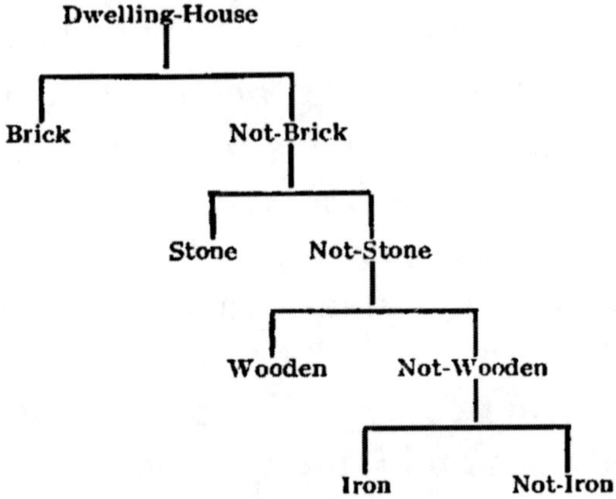

"It is quite certain that I must in this division have left a place for every possible kind of house; for if a house is not made of brick, nor stone, nor wood, nor iron, it yet comes under the species at the right hand, which is not-iron, not-wooden, not-stone, and not-brick.

. . . This manner of classifying things may seem to be inconvenient, but it is in reality the only logical way."

The student will see that the process of Classification is two-fold. The first is by Analysis, in which the Genus is divided into Species by reason of *differences*. The second is by Synthesis, in which individuals are grouped into Species, and Species into the Genus, by reason of *resemblances*. Moreover, in building up general classes, which is known as Generalization, we must first *analyze* the individual in order to ascertain its *qualities, attributes and properties,* and then *synthesize* the individual with other individuals possessing like qualities, properties or attributes.

Brooks says of Generalization: "The mind now takes the materials that have been furnished and fashioned by comparison and analysis and unites them into one single mental product, giving us the general notion or concept. The mind, as it were, brings together these several attributes into a bunch or package and then ties a mental string around it, as we would bunch a lot of roses or cigars. . . . Generalization is an *ascending* process.

The broader concept is regarded as higher than the narrower concept; a concept is considered as higher than percept; a general idea stands above a particular idea. We thus go up from particulars to generals; from percepts to concepts; from lower concepts to higher concepts. Beginning down with particular objects, we rise from them to the general idea of their class. Having formed a number of lower classes, we compare them as we did individuals and generalize them into higher classes. We perform the same process with these higher classes and thus proceed until we are at last arrested in the highest class, that of Being. Having reached the pinnacle of Generalization, we may descend the ladder by reversing the process through which we ascend."

A Concept, then, is seen to be *a general idea.* It is a general thought that embraces *all the individuals* of its own class and has in it all that is common to its own class, while it resembles *no* particular individual of its class in *all* respects. Thus, a concept of *animal* contains within itself the minor concepts of *all animals* and the animal-quality of all animals

—yet it differs from the *percept* of any one particular animal and the minor concepts of minor classes of animals. Consequently a concept or general idea cannot be *imaged* or mentally pictured. We may picture a percept of any particular thing, but we cannot picture a general idea or concept because the latter does not partake of the *particular* qualities of any of its class, but embraces all the general qualities of the class. Try to picture the general idea, or concept, of Man. You will find that any attempt to do so will result in the production of merely *a man*—some particular man. If you give the picture dark hair, it will fail to include the light-haired men; if you give it white skin, it will slight the darker-skinned races. If you picture a stout man, the thin ones are neglected. And so on in every feature. It is impossible to form a correct general class picture unless we include every individual in it. The best we can do is to form a sort of *composite* image, which at the best is in the nature of a symbol representative of the class—an ideal image to make easier the *idea* of the general class or term.

From the above we may see the fundamental differences between a Percept and a Concept. The Percept is the mental image of a real object—a particular thing. The Concept is merely a *general idea,* or general notion, of the common attributes of a class of objects or things. A Percept arises directly from sense-impressions, while a Concept is, in a sense, a pure thought—an abstract thing—a mental creation—an ideal.

A Concrete Concept is a concept embodying the common qualities of a class of objects, as for instance, the concrete concept of *lion,* in which the general class qualities of all lions are embodied. An Abstract Concept is a concept embodying merely some one quality generally diffused, as for instance, the quality of *fierceness* in the general class of lions. *Rose* is a concrete concept; *red,* or *redness,* is an abstract concept. It will aid you in remembering this distinction to memorize Jevons' rule: "*A Concrete Term is the name of a Thing; an Abstract Term is the name of a Quality of a Thing.*"

A Concrete Concept, including all the particular individuals of a class, must also contain all the common qualities of those individuals. Thus, such a concept is composed of the ideas of the particular individuals and of their common qualities, in combination and union. From this arises the distinctive terms known as the *content, extension* and *intension* of concepts, respectively.

The *content* of a concept is *all that it includes—its full meaning.* The *extension* of a concept depends upon its *quantity* aspect—it is its property of including numbers of individual objects within its content. The *intension* of a concept depends upon its *quality* aspect—it is its property of including class or common qualities, properties or attributes within its content.

Thus, the *extension* of the concept *horse* covers all individual horses; while its *intension* includes all qualities, attributes, and properties common to all horses—class qualities possessed by all horses in common, and which qualities, etc., make the particular animals *horses,* as distinguished from other animals.

It follows that the larger the number of particular objects in a class, the smaller must be the number of general class qualities—qualities common to all in the class. And, that the larger the number of common class qualities, the smaller must be the number of individuals in the class. As the logicians express it, "the greater the extension, the less the intension; the greater the intension, the less the extension." Thus, *animal* is narrow in intension, but very broad in extension; for while there are many animals there are but very few qualities common to *all* animals. And, *horse* is narrower in extension, but broader in intension; for while there are comparatively few horses, the qualities common to all horses are greater.

The cultivation of the faculty of Generalization, or Conception, of course, depends largely upon *exercise* and *material,* as does the cultivation of every mental faculty, as we have seen. But there are certain rules, methods and ideas which may be used to advantage in developing this faculty in the direction of clear and capable work. This faculty is developed by all of the general processes of thought, for it forms an important part of all thought. But the logical processes known as Analysis and Synthesis give to this faculty exercise and employment particularly adapted to its development and cultivation. Let us briefly consider these processes.

Logical Analysis is the process by which we examine and unfold the meaning of Terms. A Term, you remember, is the verbal expression of a Concept. In such analysis we endeavor to unfold and discover the *quality-aspect* and the *quantity-aspect* of the content of the concept. We seek, thereby, to discover the particular general idea expressed; the number of particular individuals included therein; and the properties of the class or generalization. Analysis depends upon division and separation. Development in the process of Logical Analysis tends toward clearness, distinctness, and exactness in thought and expression. Logical Analysis has two aspects or phases, as follows: (1) *Division,* or the separation of a concept according to its *extension,* as for instance the analysis of a genus into its various species; and (2) *Partition,* or the separation of a concept into its component qualities, properties and attributes, as for instance, the analysis of the concept *iron* into its several qualities of color, weight, hardness, malleability, tenacity, utility, etc.

There are certain rules of Division which should be observed, the following being a simple statement of the same:

I. *The division should be governed by a uniform principle.* For instance it would be illogical to first divide men into Caucasians, Mongolians, etc., and then further sub-divide them into Christians, Pagans, etc., for the first division would be according to the principle of race, and the second according to the principle of religion. Observing the rule of the "uniform principle" we may divide men into races, and sub-races, and so on, without regard to religion; and we may likewise divide men according to their respective religions, and then into minor denominations and sects, without regard to race or nationality. The above rule is frequently violated by careless thinkers and speakers.

II. *The division should be complete and exhaustive.* For instance, the analysis of a genus should extend to every known species of it, upon the principle that *the genus is merely the sum of its several species.* A textbook illustration of a violation of this rule is given in the case of the concept *actions,* when divided into *good-actions* and *bad-actions,* but omitting the very important species of *indifferent-actions.* Carelessness in observance of this rule leads to fallacious reasoning and cloudy thinking.

III. *The division should be in logical sequence.* It is illogical to skip or pass over intermediate divisions, as for instance, when we divide *animals* into *horses, trout and swallows,* omitting the intermediate division into *mammals, fish and birds.* The more perfect the sequence, the clearer the analysis and the thought resulting therefrom.

IV. *The division should be exclusive.* That is, the various species divided from a genus, should be reciprocally exclusive—should exclude one another. Thus to divide *mankind* into *male, men and women,* would be illogical, because the class *male* includes *men.* The division should be either: "*male and female;*" or else: "men, women, boys, girls."

The exercise of Division along these lines, and according to these rules, will tend to improve one's powers of conception and analysis. Any class of objects—any general concept—may be used for practice. A trial will show you the great powers of unfoldment contained within this simple process. It tends to broaden and widen one's conception of almost any class of objects.

There are also several rules for Partition which should be observed, as follows:

I. *The partition should be complete and exhaustive.* That is, it should unfold the full meaning of the term or concept, so far as is concerned its several general qualities, properties and attributes. But this applies only to the qualities, properties and attributes which are *common* to the class or concept, and not to the minor qualities which belong solely to the various sub-divisions composing the class; nor to the accidental or individual qualities belonging to the separate individuals in any sub-class. The qualities should be *essential* and not *accidental*—general, not particular. A famous violation of this rule was had in the case of the ancient Platonic definition of "Man" as: "A two-legged animal without feathers," which Diogenes rendered absurd by offering a plucked chicken as a "man" according to the definition. Clearness in thought requires the recognition of the distinction between the general qualities and the individual, particular or accidental qualities. Red-hair is an accidental quality of a particular man and not a general quality of the class *man.*

II. *The partition should consider the qualities, properties and attributes,* according to the classification of logical division. That is, the various qualities, properties and attributes should be considered in the form of genus and species, as in Division. In this classification, the rules of Division apply.

It will be seen that there is a close relationship existing between Partition and Definition. Definition is really a statement of the various qualities, attributes, and properties of a concept, either stated in particular or else in concepts of other and larger classes. There is perhaps no better exercise for the cultivation of clear thought and conception than Definition. In order to define, one must exercise his power of analysis to a considerable extent. Brooks says: "Exercises in logical definition are valuable in unfolding our conception.

Logical definition, including both the genus and the specific difference, gives clearness, definiteness and adequacy to our conceptions. It separates a conception from all other conceptions by fixing upon and presenting the essential and distinctive property or properties of the conception defined. The value of exercises in logical definition is thus readily apparent."

If the student will select some familiar term and endeavor to define it correctly, writing down the result, and will then compare the latter with the definition given in some standard dictionary, he will see a new light regarding logical definition. Practice in definition, conducted along these lines, will cultivate the powers of analysis and conception and will, at the same time, tend toward the acquiring of correct and scientific methods of thought and clear expression.

Hyslop gives the following excellent Rules of Logical Definition, which should be followed by the student in his exercises:

"I. A definition should state the essential attributes of the species defined.

"II. A definition must not contain the name

or word defined. Otherwise the definition is called *a circulus in definiendo* (defining in a circle).

"III. The definition must be exactly equivalent to the species defined.

"IV. A definition should not be expressed in obscure, figurative or ambiguous language.

"V. A definition must not be negative when it can be affirmative."

Logical Synthesis is the exact opposite of Logical Analysis. In the latter we strive to separate and take apart; in the former we strive to bind together and combine the particulars into the general. Beginning with individual things and comparing them with each other according to observed points of resemblance, we proceed to group them into species or narrow classes. These classes, or species, we then combine with similar ones, into a larger class or genus; and then, according to the same process, into broader classes as we have shown in the first part of this chapter.

The process of Synthesis is calculated to develop and cultivate the mind in several directions and exercises along these lines will give a new habit and sense of orderly arrangement, which will be most useful to the student in his every-day life. Halleck says: "Whenever a person is comparing a specimen to see whether it may be put in the same class with other specimens, he is *thinking*. Comparison is an absolutely essential factor of thought, and classification demands comparison. The man who has not properly classified the myriad individual objects with which he has to deal, must advance like a cripple. He, only, can travel with seven-league boots, who has thought out the relations existing between these stray individuals and put them into their proper classes. In a minute a business man may put his hand on any one of ten thousand letters if they are properly classified. In the same way, the student of history, sociology or any other branch, can, if he studies the subjects aright, have all his knowledge classified and speedily available for use. . . . In this way, we may make our knowledge of the world more minutely exact. We cannot classify without seeing things under a new aspect."

The study of Natural History, in any or all of its branches, will do much to cultivate the power of Classification. But one may practice classification with the objects around him in his every-day life. Arranging things mentally, into small classes, and these into larger, one will soon be able to form a logical connection between particular ideas and general ideas; particular objects and general classes. The practice of classification gives to the mind a constructive turn—a "building-up" tendency, which is most desirable in these days of construction and development. Regarding some of the pitfalls of classification, Jevons says:

"In classifying things, we must take great care not to be misled by outward resemblances. Things may seem to be very much like each other which are not so. Whales, porpoises, seals and several other animals live in the sea exactly like fish; they have a similar shape and are usually classed among fish. People are said to go whale-fishing. Yet these animals are not really fish at all, but are much more like dogs and horses and other quadrupeds than they are like fish. They cannot live entirely under water and breathe the air contained in the water like fish, but they have to come up to the surface at intervals to take breath. Similarly, we must not class bats with birds because they fly about, although they have what would be called wings; these wings are not like those of birds and in truth bats are much more like rats and mice than they are like birds. Botanists used at one time to classify plants according to their size, as trees, shrubs or herbs, but we now know that a great tree is often more similar in its character to a tiny herb than it is to other great trees. A daisy has little resemblance to a great Scotch thistle; yet the botanist regards them as very similar. The lofty growing bamboo is a kind of grass, and the sugar-cane also belongs to the same class with wheat and oats."

Remember that analysis of a genus into its component species is accomplished by a separation according to *differences;* and species are built up by synthesis into a genus because of *resemblances.* The same is true regarding individual and species, building up in accordance to points of resemblance, while analysis or separation is according to points of difference.

The use of a good dictionary will be advantageous to the student in developing the power of Generalization or Conception. Starting with a species, he may build up to higher and still higher classes by consulting the dictionary; likewise, starting with a large class, he may work down to the several species composing it. An encyclopedia, of course, is still better for the purpose in many cases. Remember that Generalization is a prime requisite for clear, logical thinking. Moreover, it is a great developer of Thought.

CHAPTER XI.

JUDGMENT

We have seen that in the several mental processes which are grouped together under the general head of Understanding, the stage or step of Abstraction is first; following which is the second step or phase, called Generalization or Conception. The third step or phase is that which is called Judgment. In the exercise of the faculty of Judgment, we determine the agreement or disagreement between two concepts, ideas, or objects of thought, by comparing them one with another. From this process of comparison arises the Judgment, which is expressed in the shape of a logical Proposition. A certain form of Judgment must be used, however, in the actual formation of a Concept, for we must first compare qualities, and make a judgment thereon, in order to form a general idea. In this place, however, we shall confine ourselves to the consideration of the faculty of Judgment in the strictly logical usage of the term, as previously stated.

We have seen that the expression of a concept is called a Term, which is the *name* of the concept. In the same way when we compare two terms (expressions of concepts) and pass Judgment thereon, the expression of that Judgment is called a Proposition. In every Judgment and Propositon there must be two Terms or Concepts, connected by a little word "is" or "are," or some form of the verb "to be," in the present tense indicative. This connecting word is called the Copula. For instance, we may compare the two terms *horse* and *animal,* as follows: "A horse is an animal," the word *is* being the Copula or symbol of the *affirmative* Judgment, which connects the two terms. In the same way we may form a *negative* Judgment as follows: "A horse is not a cow." In a Proposition, *the term of which something is affirmed* is called the Subject; and *the term expressing that which is affirmed of the subject* is called the Predicate.

Besides the distinction between affirmative Judgments, or Propositions, there is a distinction arising from *quantity,* which separates them into the respective classes of *particular* and *universal.* Thus, "*all* horses are animals," is a *universal* Judgment; while "*some* horses are black" is a particular Judgment. Thus all Judgments must be either *affirmative* or *negative*; and also either *particular* or *universal.* This gives us four possible classes of Judgments, as follows, and illustrated symbolically:

1. Universal Affirmative, as "All A is B."
2. Universal Negative, as "No A is B."
3. Particular Affirmative, as "Some A is B."
4. Particular Negative, as "Some A is not B."

The Term or Judgment is said to be "*distributed*" (that is, extended universally) when it is used in its fullest sense, in which it is used in the sense of "each and every" of its kind or class. Thus in the proposition "Horses are animals" the meaning is that "*each and every*" horse is an animal—in this case the *subject* is "distributed" or made universal. But the *predicate* is *not* "distributed" or made universal, but remains particular or restricted and implies merely "some." For the proposition does not mean that the class "*horses*" includes *all* animals. For we may say that: "*Some* animals are *not* horses." So you see we have several instances in which the "distribution" varies, both as regards the subject and also the predicate. The rule of logic applying in this case is as follows:

1. In *universal* propositions, the *subject* is distributed.
2. In *particular* propositions, the *subject* is *not* distributed.
3. In *negative* propositions, the *predicate* is distributed.
4. In *affirmative* propositions, the *predicate* is *not* distributed.

A little time devoted to the analysis and understanding of the above rules will repay the student for his trouble, inasmuch as it will train his mind in the direction of logical distinction and judgment. The importance of these rules will appear later.

Halleck says: "Judgment is the power revolutionizing the world. The revolution is slow because nature's forces are so complex, so hard to be reduced to their simplest forms, and so disguised and neutralized by the presence of other forces. The progress of the next hundred years will join many concepts, which now seem to have no common qualities. If the vast amount of energy latent in the sunbeams, in the rays of the stars, in the winds, in the rising and falling of the tides, is treasured up and applied to human purposes, it will be a fresh triumph for judgment. This world is rolling around in a universe of energy, of which judgment has as yet harnessed only the smallest appreciable fraction. Fortunately, judgment is ever working and silently comparing things that, to past ages, have seemed dissimilar; and it is constantly abstracting and leaving out of the field of view those qualities which have simply served to obscure the point at issue." Brooks says: "The power of judgment is of great value to its products. It is involved in or accompanies every act of the intellect, and thus lies at the foundation of all intellectual activity. It operates directly in every act of the understanding; and even aids the other faculties of the mind in completing their activities and products."

The best method of cultivating the power of Judgment is the exercise of the faculty in the direction of making comparisons, of weighing differences and resemblances, and in generally training the mind along the lines of Logical Thinking. Another volume of this series is devoted to the latter subject, and should aid the student who wishes to cultivate the habit of logical and scientific thought. The study of mathematics is calculated to develop the faculty of Judgment, because it necessitates the use of the powers of comparison and decision. Mental arithmetic, especially, will tend to strengthen, and exercise this faculty of the mind.

Geometry and Logic will give the very best exercise along these lines to those who care to devote the time, attention and work to the task. Games, such as chess, and checkers or draughts, tend to develop the powers of Judgment. The study of the definitions of words in a good dictionary will also tend to give excellent exercise along the same lines. The exercises given in this book for the cultivation and development of the several faculties, will tend to develop this particular faculty in a general way, for the exercise of Judgment is required at each step of the way, and in each exercise.

Brooks says: "It should be one of the leading objects of the culture of young people to lead them to acquire the habit of forming judgments. They should not only be led to see things, but to have opinions about things. They should be trained to see things in their relations, and to put these relations into definite propositions. Their ideas of objects should be worked up into thoughts concerning the objects. Those methods of teaching are best which tend to excite a thoughtful habit of mind that notices the similitudes and diversities of objects, and endeavors to read the thoughts which they embody and of which they are the symbols."

The exercises given at the close of the next chapter, entitled "Derived Judgments," will give to the mind a decided trend in the direction of logical judgment. We heartily recommend them to the student.

The student will find that he will tend to acquire the habit of clear logical comparison and judgment, if he will memorize and apply in his thinking the following excellent *Primary Rules of Thought*, stated by Jevons:

"I. *Law of Identity*: The same quality or thing is *always* the same quality or thing, no matter how different the conditions in which it occurs.

"II. *Law of Contradiction*: Nothing can at the same time and place *both* be and not be.

"III. *Law of Excluded Middle*: Everything must *either* be, or not be; there is no other alternative or middle course."

Jevons says of these laws: "Students are seldom able to see at first their full meaning and importance. All arguments may be explained when these self-evident laws are granted; and it is not too much to say that *the whole of logic will be plain to those who will constantly use these laws as their key.*"

CHAPTER XII.

DERIVED JUDGMENTS

As we have seen, a Judgment is obtained by comparing two objects of thought according to their agreement or difference. The next higher step, that of logical Reasoning, consists of the comparing of two ideas through their relation to a third. This form of reasoning is called *mediate*, because it is effected through the *medium* of the third idea. There is, however, a certain process of Understanding which comes in between this mediate reasoning on the one hand, and the formation of a plain judgment on the other. Some authorities treat it as a form of *reasoning*, calling it *Immediate Reasoning* or Immediate Inference, while others treat it as a higher form of Judgment, calling it Derived Judgment. We shall follow the latter classification, as best adapted for the particular purposes of this book.

The fundamental principle of Derived Judgment is that ordinary Judgments are often so related to each other that one Judgment may be derived directly and immediately from another. The two particular forms of the general method of Derived Judgment are known as those of (1) Opposition; and (2) Conversion; respectively.

In order to more clearly understand the logical processes involved in Derived Judgment, we should acquaint ourselves with the general relations of Judgments, and with the symbolic letters used by logicians as a means of simplifying the processes of thought. Logicians denote each of the four classes of Judgments or Propositions by a certain letter, the first four vowels—A, E, I and O, being used for the purpose. It has been found very convenient to use these symbols in denoting the various forms of Propositions and Judgments. The following table should be memorized for this purpose:

Universal Affirmative, symbolized by "A."
Universal Negative, symbolized by "E."
Particular Affirmative, symbolized by "I."
Particular Negative, symbolized by "O."

It will be seen that these four forms of Judgments bear certain relations to each other, from which arises what is called opposition. This may be better understood by reference to the following table called the Square of Opposition:

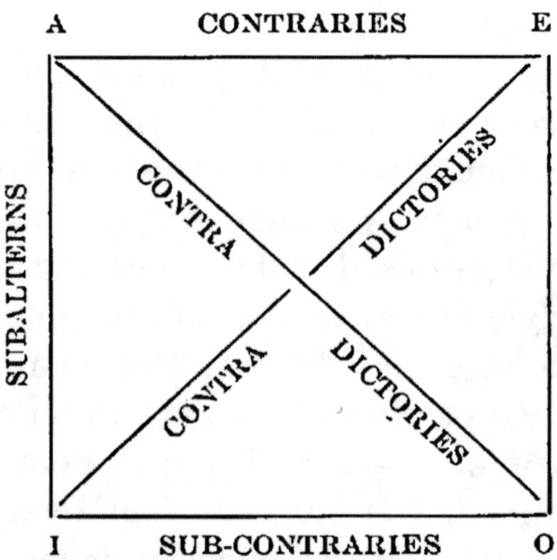

Thus, A and E are *contraries*; I and O are *sub-contraries*; A and I, and also E and O are subalterns; A and O, and also E and I are *contradictories.*

The following will give a symbolic table of each of the four Judgments or Propositions with the logical symbols attached:

(A) "All A is B."

(E) "No A is B."

(I) "Some A is B."

(O) "Some A is not B."

The following are the rules governing and expressing the relations above indicated:

I. Of the Contradictories: *One must be true, and the other must be false.* As for instance, (A) "All A is B;" and (O) "Some A is not B;" cannot both be true at the same time. Neither can (E) "No A is B;" and (I) "Some A is B;" both be true at the same time. They are *contradictory* by nature,—and if one is true, the other must be false; if one is false, the other must be true.

II. Of the Contraries: *If one is true the other must be false; but, both may be false.* As for instance, (A) "All A is B;" and (E) "No A is B;" cannot both be true at the same time. If one is true the other *must* be false. *But*, both may be *false*, as we may see when we find we may state that (I) "*Some* A is B." So while these two propositions are *contrary*, they are not *contradictory*. While, if one of them is *true* the other must be false, it does not follow that if one is *false* the other must be *true*, for both *may be false*, leaving the truth to be found in a third proposition.

III. Of the Subcontraries: *If one is false the other must be true; but both may be true.* As for instance, (I) "Some A is B;" and (O) "Some A is not B;" may both be true, for they do not contradict each other. But one or the other must be true—they can not both be false.

IV. Of the Subalterns: *If the Universal (A or E) be true the Particular (I or O) must be true.* As for instance, if (A) "All A is B" is true, then (I) "Some A is B" must also be true; also, if (E) "No A is B" is true, then "Some A is not B" must also be true. The Universal carries the particular within its truth and meaning. But; *If the Universal is false, the particular may be true or it may be false.* As for instance (A) "All A is B" may be false, and yet (I) "Some A is B" may be either true or false, without being determined by the (A) proposition. And, likewise, (E) "No A is B" may be false without determining the truth or falsity of (O) "Some A is not B."

But: *If the Particular be false, the Universal also must be false.* As for instance, if (I) "Some A is B" is false, then it must follow that (A) "All A is B" must also be false; or if (O) "Some A is not B" is false, then (E) "No A is B" must also be false. But: *The Particular may be true, without rendering the Universal true.* As for instance: (I) "*Some* A is B" may be true without making true (A) "*All* A is B;" or (O) "Some A is not B" may be true without making true (E) "No A is B."

The above rules may be worked out not only with the symbols, as "All A is B," but also with *any* Judgments or Propositions, such as "All horses are animals;" "All men are mortal;" "Some men are artists;" etc. The principle involved is identical in each and every case. The "All A is B" symbology is merely adopted for simplicity, and for the purpose of rendering the logical process akin to that of mathematics. The letters play the same part that the numerals or figures do in arithmetic or the *a, b, c; x, y, z,* in algebra. Thinking in symbols tends toward clearness of thought and reasoning.

Exercise: Let the student apply the principles of Opposition by using any of the above judgments mentioned in the preceding paragraph, in the direction of erecting a Square of Opposition of them, after having attached the symbolic letters A, E, I and O, to the appropriate forms of the propositions.

Then let him work out the following problems from the Tables and Square given in this chapter.

1. If "A" is true; show what follows for E, I and O. Also what follows if "A" be *false.*

2. If "E" is true; show what follows for A, I and O. Also what follows if "E" be *false.*

3. If "I" is true; show what follows for A, E and O. Also what follows if "E" be *false.*

4. If "O" is true; show what follows for A, E and I. Also what happens if "O" be *false.*

CONVERSION OF JUDGMENTS

Judgments are capable of the process of Conversion, or *the change of place of subject and predicate.* Hyslop says: "Conversion is the transposition of subject and predicate, or the process of immediate inference by which we can infer from a given preposition another having the predicate of the original for its subject, and the subject of the original for its predicate." The process of converting a proposition seems simple at first thought but a little consideration will show that there are many difficulties in the way. For instance, while it is a true judgment that "All *horses* are *animals*," it is not a correct Derived Judgment or Inference that "All *animals* are *horses*. The same is true of the possible conversion of the judgment "All biscuit is bread" into that of "All bread is biscuit." There are certain rules to be observed in Conversion, as we shall see in a moment.

The Subject of a judgment is, of course, *the term of which something is affirmed*; and the Predicate is *the term expressing that which is affirmed of the Subject*. The Predicate is really an expression of an *attribute* of the Subject. Thus when we say "All horses are animals" we express the idea that *all horses* possess the *attribute* of "animality;" or when we say that "Some men are artists," we express the idea that *some men* possess the *attributes* or qualities included in the concept "artist." In Conversion, the original judgment is called the Convertend; and the new form of judgment, resulting from the conversion, is called the Converse. Remember these terms, please.

The two Rules of Conversion, stated in simple form, are as follows:

I. Do not change the quality of a judgment. The quality of the converse must remain the same as that of the convertend.

II. Do not distribute an undistributed term. No term must be distributed in the converse which is not distributed in the convertend.

The reason of these rules is that it would be contrary to truth and logic to give to a converted judgment a higher degree of quality and quantity than is found in the original judgment. To do so would be to attempt to make "twice 2" more than "2 plus 2."

There are three methods or kinds of Conversion, as follows: (1) Simple Conversion; (2) Limited Conversion; and (3) Conversion by Contraposition.

In Simple Conversion, there is no change in either quality or quantity. For instance, by Simple Conversion we may convert a proposition by changing the places of its subject and predicate, respectively. But as Jevons says: "It does not follow that the new one will always be true if the old one was true. Sometimes this is the case, and sometimes it is not. If I say, 'some churches are wooden-buildings,' I may turn it around and get 'some wooden-buildings are churches;' the meaning is exactly the same as before. This kind of change is called Simple Conversion, because we need do nothing but simply change the subjects and predicates in order to get a new proposition. We see that the Particular Affirmative proposition can be simply converted. Such is the case also with the Universal Negative proposition. 'No large flowers are green things' may be converted simply into 'no green things are large flowers.' "

In Limited Conversion, the quantity is changed from Universal to Particular. Of this, Jevons continues: "But it is a more troublesome matter, however, to convert a Universal Affirmative proposition. The statement that 'all jelly fish are animals,' is true; but, if we convert it, getting 'all animals are jelly fish,' the result is absurd. This is because the predicate of a universal proposition is really particular. We do not mean that jelly fish are 'all' the animals which exist, but only 'some' of the animals. The proposition ought really to be 'all jelly fish are *some* animals,' and if we converted this simply, we should get, 'some animals are all jelly fish.' But we almost always leave out the little adjectives *some* and *all* when they would occur in the predicate, so that the proposition, when converted, becomes '*some* animals are jelly fish.' This kind of change is called Limited Conversion, and we see that a Universal Affirmative proposition, when so converted, gives a Particular Affirmative one."

In Conversion by Contraposition, there is a change in the position of the negative copula, which shifts the expression of the quality. As for instance, in the Particular Negative "Some animals are not horses," we cannot say "Some horses are not animals," for that would be a violation of the rule that "no term must be distributed in the converse which is not distributed in the convertend," for as we have seen in the preceding chapter: "In Particular propositions the *subject* is *not* distributed." And in the original proposition, or convertend, "animals" is the *subject* of a Particular proposition. Avoiding this, and proceeding by Conversion by Contraposition, we convert the Convertend (O) into a Particular Affirmative (I), saying: "Some animals are not-horses;" or "Some animals are things not horses;" and then proceeding by Simple Conversion we get the converse, "Some things not horses are animals," or "Some not-horses are animals."

The following gives the application of the appropriate form of Conversion to each of the several four kind of Judgments or Propositions:

(A) *Universal Affirmative*: This form of proposition is converted by Limited Conversion. The predicate not being distributed in the convertend, it cannot be distributed in the converse, by saying "all." ("In affirmative propositions the *predicate* is *not* distributed.") Thus by this form of Conversion, we convert "All horses are animals" into "Some animals are horses." The Universal Affirmative (A) is converted by limitation into a Particular Affirmative (I).

(E) *Universal Negative*: This form of proposition is converted by Simple Conversion. In a Universal Negative *both terms are distributed.* ("In universal propositions, the *subject* is distributed;" "In negative propositions, the *predicate* is distributed.") So we may say "No cows are horses," and then convert the proposition into "No horses are cows." We simply convert one Universal Negative (E) into another Universal Negative (E).

(I) *Particular Affirmative*: This form of proposition is converted by Simple Conversion. For *neither term is distributed* in a Particular Affirmative. ("In particular propositions, the *subject* is *not* distributed. In affirmative propositions, the *predicate* is *not* distributed.") And neither term being distributed in the convertend, it must not be distributed in the converse. So from "Some horses are males" we may by Simple Conversion derive "Some males are horses." We simply convert one Particular Affirmative (I), into another Particular Affirmative (I).

(O) *Particular Negative*: This form of proposition is converted by Contraposition or Negation. We have given examples and illustrations in the paragraph describing Conversion by Contraposition. The Particular Negative (I) is converted by contraposition into a Particular Affirmative (I) which is then simply converted into another Particular Affirmative (I).

There are several minor processes or methods of deriving judgments from each other, or of making immediate inferences, but the above will give the student a very fair idea of the minor or more complete methods.

Exercise: The following will give the student good practice and exercise in the methods of Conversion. It affords a valuable mental drill, and tends to develop the logical faculties, particularly that of Judgment. The student should *convert* the following propositions, according to the rules and examples given in this chapter:

1 All men are reasoning beings.
2. Some men are blacksmiths.
3. No men are quadrupeds.
4. Some birds are sparrows.
5. Some horses are vicious.
6. No brute is rational.
7. Some men are not sane.
8. All biscuit is bread.
9. Some bread is biscuit.
10. Not all bread is biscuit.

CHAPTER XIII

REASONING

In the preceding chapters we have seen that in the group of mental processes involved in the general process of Understanding, there are several stages or steps, three of which we have considered in turn, namely: (1) Abstraction; (2) Generalization or Conception; (3) Judgment. The *fourth* step, or stage, and the one which we are now about to consider, is that called Reasoning.

Reasoning is that faculty of the mind whereby we compare two Judgments, one with the other, and from which comparison we are enabled to form a third judgment. It is a form of indirect or mediate comparison, whereas, the ordinary Judgment is a form of immediate or direct comparison. As, when we form a Judgment, we compare two concepts and decide upon their agreement or difference; so in Reasoning we compare two Judgments and from the comparison we draw or produce a new Judgment. Thus, we may reason that the particular dog "Carlo" is an animal, by the following process:

(1) *All* dogs are animals; (2) Carlo is a dog; therefore, (3) Carlo is an animal. Or, in the same way, we may reason that a whale is not a fish, as follows:

(1) *All* fish are cold-blooded animals; (2) A whale is *not* a cold-blooded animal; therefore, (3) A whale is *not* a fish.

In the above processes it will be seen that the third and final Judgment is derived from a comparison of the first two Judgments. Brooks states the process as follows: "Looking at the process more closely, it will be seen that in inference in Reasoning involves a comparison of relations. We infer the relation of two objects from their relation to a third object. We must thus grasp in the mind two relations and from the comparison of these two relations we infer a third relation. The two relations from which we infer a third, are judgments; hence, Reasoning may also be defined as the process of deriving one judgment from two other judgments. We compare the two given judgments and from this comparison derive the third judgment. This constitutes a single step in Reasoning, and an argument so expressed is called a *Syllogism.*"

The *Syllogism* consists of three propositions, the first two of which express the grounds or basis of the argument and are called the *premises;* the third expresses the inference derived from a comparison of the other two and is called the *conclusion.* We shall not enter into a technical consideration of the Syllogism in this book, as the subject is considered in detail in the volume of this series devoted to the subject of "Logic." Our concern here is to point out the natural process and course of Reasoning, rather than to consider the technical features of the process.

Reasoning is divided into two general classes, known respectively as (1) *Inductive Reasoning;* (2) *Deductive Reasoning.*

Inductive Reasoning is the process of arriving at a general truth, law or principle from a consideration of many particular facts and truths. Thus, if we find that a certain thing is true of a great number of particular objects, we may infer that the same thing is true of *all* objects of this particular kind. In one of the examples given above, one of the judgments was that "all fish are cold-blooded animals," which general truth was arrived at by Inductive Reasoning based upon the examination of a great number of fish, and from thence assuming that *all* fish are true to this general law of truth.

Deductive Reasoning is the reverse of Inductive Reasoning, and is a process of arriving at a particular truth from the assumption of a general truth. Thus, from the assumption that "all fish are cold-blooded animals," we, by Deductive Reasoning, arrive at the conclusion that the particular fish before us must be cold-blooded.

Inductive Reasoning proceeds upon the basic principle that "*What is true of the many is true of the whole,*" while Deductive Reasoning proceeds upon the basic principle that "*What is true of the whole is true of its parts.*"

Regarding the principle of *Inductive Reasoning,* Halleck says: "Man has to find out through his own experience, or that of others, the major premises from which he argues or draws his conclusions. By induction, we examine what seems to us a sufficient number of individual cases. We then conclude that the rest of these cases, which we have not examined, will obey the same general law. The judgment 'All men are mortal' was reached by induction. It was observed that all past generations of men had died, and this fact warranted the conclusion that all men living will die. We make that assertion as boldly as if we had seen them all die. The premise, 'All cows chew the cud,' was laid down after a certain number of cows had been examined. If we were to see a cow twenty years hence, we should expect to find that she chewed the cud. It was noticed by astronomers that, after a certain number of days, the earth regularly returned to the same position in its orbit, the sun rose in the same place, and the day was of the same length. Hence, the length of the year and of each succeeding day was determined, and the almanac maker now infers that the same will be true of future years. He tells us that the sun on the first of next December will rise at a given time, although he cannot throw himself into the future to verify the conclusion."

Brooks says regarding this principle: "This

proposition is founded on our faith in the uniformity of nature; take away this belief, and all reasoning by induction fails. The basis of induction is thus often stated to be *man's faith in the uniformity of nature.* Induction has been compared to a ladder upon which we ascend from facts to laws. This ladder cannot stand unless it has something to rest upon; and this something is our faith in the constancy of nature's laws."

There are two general ways of obtaining our basis for the process of Inductive Reasoning. One of these is called Perfect Induction and the other Imperfect Induction. Perfect Induction is possible only when we have had the opportunity of examining every particular object or thing of which the general idea is expressed. For instance, if we could examine every fish in the universe we would have the basis of Perfect Induction for asserting the general truth that "all fishes are cold-blooded." But this is practically impossible in the great majority of cases, and so we must fall back upon more or less Imperfect Induction. We must assume the general law from the fact that it is seen to exist in a very great number of particular cases; upon the principle that "What is true of the many is true of the whole." As Halleck says regarding this: "Whenever we make a statement such as, 'All men are mortal,' without having tested each individual case or, in other words, without having seen every man die, we are reasoning from *imperfect* induction. Every time a man buys a piece of beef, a bushel of potatoes or a loaf of bread, he is basing his action on inference from imperfect induction. He believes that beef, potatoes and bread will prove nutritious food, although he has not actually tested those special edibles before purchasing them. They have hitherto been found to be nutritious on trial and he argues that the same will prove true of those special instances. Whenever a man takes stock in a new national bank, a manufactory or a bridge, he is arguing from past cases that this special investment will prove profitable. We instinctively believe in the uniformity of nature; if we did not we should not consult our almanacs. If sufficient heat will cause phosphorus to burn to-day, we conclude that the same result will follow to-morrow if the circumstances are the same."

But, it will be seen, much care must be exercised in making observations, experiments and comparisons, and in making generalizations. The following general principles will give the views of the authorities regarding this:

Atwater gives the two general rules:

Rule of Agreement: "If, whenever a given object or agency is present, without counteracting forces, a given effect is produced, there is a strong evidence that the object or agency is the cause of the effect."

Rule of Disagreement: "If when the supposed cause is present the effect is present, and when the supposed cause is absent the effect is wanting, there being in neither case any other agents present to effect the result, we may reasonably infer that the supposed cause is the real one."

Rule of Residue: "When in any phenomena we find a result remaining after the effects of all known causes are estimated, we may attribute it to a residual agent not yet reckoned."

Rule of Concomitant Variations: "When a variation in a given antecedent is accompanied by a variation of a given consequent, they are in some manner related as cause and effect."

Atwater says, of the above rules, that "whenever either of these criteria is found, free from conflicting evidence, and especially when several of them concur, the evidence is clear that the cases observed are fair representatives of the whole class, and warrant a valid universal inductive conclusion."

We now come to what is known as Hypothesis or Theory, which is an assumed general principle—a conjecture or supposition founded upon observed and tested facts. Some authorities use the term "theory" in the sense of "a verified hypothesis," but the two terms are employed loosely and the usage varies with different authorities. What is known as "the probability of a hypothesis" is the proportion of the number of facts it will explain. The greater the number of facts it will explain, the greater is its "probability." A Hypothesis is said to be "verified" when it will account for all the facts which are properly to be referred to it. Some very critical authorities hold that verification should also depend upon there being no other possible hypotheses which will account for the facts, but this is generally considered an extreme position.

A Hypothesis is the result of a peculiar mental process which seems to act in the direction of making a sudden anticipatory leap toward a theory, after the mind has been saturated with a great body of particular facts. Some have spoken of the process as almost *intuitive* and, indeed, the testimony of many discoverers of great natural laws would lead us to believe that the Subconscious region of the mind most active in making what La Place has called "the great guess" of discovery of principle. As Brooks says: "The forming of hypotheses requires a suggestive mind, a lively fancy, a philosophic imagination, that catches a glimpse of the idea through the form, or sees the law standing behind the fact."

Thomson says: "The system of anatomy which has immortalized the name of Oken, is the consequence of a flash of anticipation which glanced through his mind when he picked up in a chance walk the skull of a deer, bleached and disintegrated by the weather, and exclaimed, after a glance, 'It is part of a vertebral column.' When Newton saw the apple fall, the anticipatory question flashed through his mind, 'Why do not the heavenly bodies fall like this apple?' In neither case had accident any important share; Newton and Oken were prepared by the deepest previous study to seize upon the unimportant fact offered to them, and show how important it might become; and if the apple and the deer-skull had been wanting, some other falling body, or some other skull, would have touched the string so ready to vibrate. But in each case there was a great step of anticipation; Oken thought he saw the type of the whole skeleton in a single vertebra, whilst Newton conceived at once that the whole universe was full of bodies tending to fall."

Passing from the consideration of Inductive Reasoning to that of Deductive Reasoning we find ourselves confronted with an entirely opposite condition. As Brooks says: "The two methods of reasoning are the reverse of each other. One goes from particulars to generals; the other from generals to particulars. One is a process of analysis; the other is a process of synthesis. One rises from facts to laws; the other descends from laws to facts. Each is independent of the other; and each is a valid and essential method of inference."

Deductive Reasoning is, as we have seen, dependent upon the process of deriving a particular truth from a general law, principle or truth, upon the fundamental axiom that: "What is true of the whole is true of its parts." It is an analytical process, just as Inductive Reasoning is synthetical. It is a descending process, just as Inductive Reasoning is ascending.

Halleck says of Deductive Reasoning: "After induction has classified certain phenomena and thus given us a major premise, we proceed deductively to apply the inference to any new specimen that can be shown to belong to that class. Induction hands over to deduction a ready-made major premise, *e. g.* '*All scorpions are dangerous.*' Deduction takes this as a fact, making no inquiry about its truth. When a new object is presented, say a possible scorpion, the only troublesome step is to decide whether the object is really a scorpion. This may be a severe task on judgment. The average inhabitant of the temperate zone would probably not care to risk a hundred dollars on his ability to distinguish a scorpion from a centipede, or from twenty or thirty other creatures bearing some resemblance to a scorpion. Here there must be accurately formed concepts and sound judgment must be used in comparing them. As soon as we decide that the object is really a scorpion, we complete the deduction in this way:—'*All scorpions are dangerous; this creature is a scorpion; this creature is dangerous.*' The reasoning of early life must be necessarily inductive. The mind is then forming general conclusions from the examination of individual phenomena. Only after general laws have been laid down, after objects have been classified, after major premises have been formed, can deduction be employed."

What is called *Reasoning by Analogy* is really but a higher degree of Generalization. It is based upon the idea that if two or more things resemble each other in many particulars, they are apt to resemble each other in other particulars. Some have expressed the principle as follows: "Things that have some things in common have other things in common." Or as Jevons states it: "The rule for reasoning by analogy is that if two or more things resemble each other in many points, they will probably resemble each other also in more points."

This form of reasoning, while quite common and quite convenient, is also very dangerous. It affords many opportunities for making false inferences. As Jevons says: "In many cases Reasoning by Analogy is found to be a very uncertain guide. In some cases unfortunate mistakes are committed. Children are sometimes killed by gathering and eating poisonous berries, wrongly inferring that they can be eaten, because other berries, of a somewhat similar appearance, have been found agreeable and harmless. Poisonous toadstools are occasionally mistaken for mushrooms, especially by people not accustomed to gather them. . . . There is no way in which we can really assure ourselves that we are arguing safely by analogy. The only rule that can be given is this, *that the more things resemble each other, the more likely is it that they are the same in other respects, especially in points closely connected with those observed."*

Halleck says: "In argument or reasoning we are much aided by the habit of searching for hidden resemblances. We may here use the term *analogy* in the narrower sense as a resemblance of ratios. There is analogical relation between autumnal frosts and vegetation on the one hand, and death and human life on the other. Frosts stand in the same relation to vegetation that death does to life. The detection of such a relation cultivates thought. If we are to succeed in argument, we must develop what some call a sixth sense for the detection of such relations. . . . Many false analogies are manufactured and it is excellent thought training to expose them. The majority of people think so little that they swallow false analogies just as newly-fledged robins swallow small stones dropped into their open mouths. . . . The study of poetry may be made very serviceable in detecting analogies and cultivating the reasoning powers. When the poet brings clearly to mind the change due to death, using as an illustration the caterpillar body transformed into the butterfly spirit, moving with winged ease over flowing meadows, he is cultivating our apprehension of relations, none the less valuable because they are beautiful.''

There are certain studies which tend to develop the power or faculty of *Inductive Reasoning.* Any study which leads the mind to consider classification and general principles, laws or truth, will tend to develop the faculty of deduction. Physics, Chemistry, Astronomy, Biology and Natural History are particularly adapted to develop the mind in this particular direction. Moreover, the mind should be directed to an inquiry into the *causes* of *things.* Facts and phenomena should be observed and an attempt should be made not only to classify them, but also to discover general principles moving them. Tentative or provisional hypotheses should be erected and then the facts re-examined in order to see whether they support the hypotheses or theory. Study of the processes whereby the great scientific theories were erected, and the proofs then adduced in support of them, will give the mind the habit of thinking along the lines of logical induction. The question ever in the mind in Inductive Reasoning is "*Why?*" The dominant idea in Inductive Reasoning is the Search for Causes.

In regard to the pitfalls of Inductive Reasoning—the fallacies, so-called, Hyslop says: "It is not easy to indicate the inductive fallacies, if it be even possible, in the formal process of induction. . . . It is certain, however, that in respect to the subject-matter of the conclusion in inductive reasoning there are some very definite limitations upon the right to transcend the premises. We cannot infer anything we please from any premises we please. We must conform to certain definite rules or principles. Any violation of them will be a fallacy. These rules are the same as those for material fallacies in deduction, so that the fallacies of induction, whether they are ever formal or not, are at least material; that is they occur whenever equivocation and presumption are committed. There are, then, two simple rules which should not be violated. (1) The subject-matter in the conclusion should be of the same general kind as in the premises. (2) The facts constituting the premises must be accepted and must not be fictitious."

One may develop his faculty or power of *Deductive Reasoning* by pursuing certain lines of study. The study of Mathematics, particularly in its branch of Mental Arithmetic is especially valuable in this direction. Algebra and Geometry have long been known to exercise an influence over the mind which gives to it a logical trend and cast. The processes involved in Geometry are akin to those employed in Logical reasoning, and must necessarily train the mind in this special direction. As Brooks says: "So valuable is geometry as a discipline that many lawyers and others review their geometry every year in order to keep the mind drilled to logical habits of thinking." The study of Grammar, Rhetoric and the Languages, are also valuable in the culture and development of the faculty of Deductive Reasoning. The study of Psychology and Philosophy have value in this connection. The study of Law is very valuable in creating logical habits of thinking deductively.

But in the study of Logic we have possibly the best exercise in the development and culture of this particular faculty. As Brooks well says: "The study of Logic will aid in the development of the power of deductive reasoning. It does this first by showing the method by which we reason. To know how we reason, to see the laws which govern the reasoning process, to analyze the syllogism and see its conformity to the laws of thought, is not only an exercise of reasoning, but gives that knowledge of the process that will be both a stimulus and a guide to thought. No one can trace the principles and processes of thought without receiving thereby an impetus to thought. In the second place, the study of logic is probably even more valuable because it gives practice in deductive thinking. This, perhaps, is its principal value, since *the mind reasons instinctively without knowing how it reasons.* One can think without the knowledge of the science of thinking, just as one can use language correctly without a knowledge of grammar; yet as the study of grammar improves one's speech, so the study of logic cannot but improve one's thought."

The study of the common *fallacies,* such as "Begging the Question," "Reasoning in a

Circle,'' etc., is particularly important to the student, for when one realizes that such fallacies exist, and is able to detect and recognize them, he will avoid their use in framing his own arguments, and will be able to expose them when they appear in the arguments of others.

The fallacy of ''Begging the Question'' consists in assuming as a proven fact something that has not been proven, or is not accepted as proven by the other party to the argument. It is a common trick in debate. The fact assumed may be either the particular point to be proved, or the premise necessary to prove it. Hyslop gives the following illustration of this fallacy: ''*Good institutions should be united;* Church and State are good institutions; therefore, Church and State should be united.'' The above syllogism seems reasonable at first thought, but analysis will show that the major premise ''Good institutions should be united'' is a mere assumption without proof. Destroy this premise and the whole reasoning fails.

Another form of fallacy, quite common, is that called ''Reasoning in a Circle,'' which consists in assuming as proof of a proposition the proposition itself, as for instance, "This man is a rascal, *because he is a rogue;* he is a rogue, *because he is a rascal.*" "We see through glass, *because it is. transparent.*" "The child is dumb, *because it has lost the power of speech.*" "He is untruthful, *because he is a liar.*" "The weather is warm, *because it is summer;* it is summer, *because the weather is warm.*"

These and other fallacies may be detected by a knowledge of Logic, and the perception and detection of them strengthens one in his faculty of Deductive Reasoning. The study of the Laws of the Syllogism, in Logic, will give to one a certain habitual sense of stating the terms of his argument according to these laws, which when acquired will be a long step in the direction of logical thinking, and the culture of the faculties of deductive reasoning.

In concluding this chapter, we wish to call your attention to a fact often overlooked by the majority of people. Halleck well expresses it as follows: "Belief is a mental state which might as well be classed under *emotion* as under thinking, for it combines both elements. Belief is a part inference from the known to the unknown, and part feeling and emotion." Others have gone so far as to say that the majority of people employ their intellects merely to *prove* to themselves and others that which they *feel to be true,* or *wish to be true,* rather than to ascertain what is *actually true* by logical methods. Others have said that "men do not require *arguments* to convince them; they want only *excuses* to justify them in their feelings, desires or actions." Cynical though this may seem, there is sufficient truth in it to warn one to guard against the tendency.

Jevons says, regarding the question of the culture of logical processes of thought: "Monsieur Jourdain, an amusing person in one of Moliere's plays, expressed much surprise on learning that he had been talking prose for more than forty years without knowing it. Ninety-nine people out of a hundred might be equally surprised on hearing that they had long been converting propositions, syllogizing, falling into paralogisms, framing hypotheses and making classifications with genera and species. If asked if they were logicians, they would probably answer, No. They would be partly right; for I believe that a large number even of educated persons have no clear idea of what logic is. Yet, in a certain way, every one must have been a logician since he began to speak. It may be asked:—If we cannot help being logicians, why do we need logic books at all? The answer is that there are logicians, and *logicians*. All persons are logicians in some manner or degree; but unfortunately many people are bad ones and suffer harm in consequence. It is just the same in other matters. Even if we do not know the meaning of the name, we are all *athletes* in some manner or degree. No one can climb a tree or get over a gate without being more or less an athlete. Nevertheless, he who wishes to do these actions really well, to have a strong muscular frame and thereby to secure good health and personal safety, as far as possible, should learn athletic exercises."

CHAPTER XIV.

CONSTRUCTIVE IMAGINATION

From the standpoint of the old psychology, a chapter bearing the above title would be considered quite out of place in a book on Thought-Culture, the Imagination being considered as outside the realm of practical psychology, and as belonging entirely to the idealistic phase of mental activities. The popular idea concerning the Imagination also is opposed to the "practical" side of its use. In the public mind the Imagination is regarded as something connected with idle dreaming and fanciful mental imaging. Imagination is considered as almost synonomous with "Fancy."

But the New Psychology sees beyond this negative phase of the Imagination and recognizes the positive side which is essentially constructive when backed up with a determined will. It recognizes that while the Imagination is by its very nature *idealistic*, yet these ideals may be made real—these subjective pictures may be materialized objectively. The positive phase of the Imagination manifests in planning, designing, projecting, mapping out, and in general in erecting the mental framework which is afterward clothed with the material structure of actual accomplishment. And, accordingly, it has seemed to us that a chapter on "Constructive Imagination" might well conclude this book on Thought-Culture.

Halleck says: "It was once thought that the imagination should be repressed, not cultivated, that it was in the human mind like weeds in a garden. . . In this age there is no mental power that stands more in need of cultivation than the imagination. So practical are its results that a man without it cannot possibly be a good plumber. He must image short cuts for placing his pipe. The image of the direction to take to elude an obstacle must precede the actual laying of the pipe. If he fixes it before traversing the way with his imagination, he frequently gets into trouble and has to tear down his work. Some one has said that the more imagination a blacksmith has, the better will he shoe a horse. Every time he strikes the red-hot iron, he makes it approximate to the image in his mind. Nor is this image a literal copy of the horse's foot. If there is a depression in that, the imagination must build out a corresponding elevation in the image, and the blows must make the iron fit the image."

Brodie says: "Physical investigation, more than anything else, helps to teach us the actual value and right use of the imagination—of that wondrous faculty, which, when left to ramble uncontrolled, leads us astray into a wilderness of perplexities and errors, a land of mists and shadows; but which, properly controlled by experience and reflection, becomes the noblest attribute of man, the source of poetic genius, the instrument of discovery in science, without the aid of which Newton would never have invented fluxions nor Davy have decomposed the earths and alkalies, nor would Columbus have found another continent.

The Imagination is more than Memory, for the latter merely reproduces the impressions made upon it, while the Imagination gathers up the material of impression and weaves new fabrics from them or builds new structures from their separated units. As Tyndall well said: "Philosophers may be right in affirming that we cannot transcend experience; but we can at all events carry it a long way from its origin. We can also magnify, diminish, qualify and combine experiences, so as to render them fit for purposes entirely new. We are gifted with the power of imagination and by this power we can lighten the darkness which surrounds the world of the senses. There are tories, even in science, who regard imagination as a faculty to be feared and avoided rather than employed. But bounded and conditioned by cooperant reason, imagination becomes the mightiest instrument of the physical discoverer. Newton's passage from a falling apple to a falling moon was, at the outset, a leap of the imagination."

Brooks says: "The imagination is a creative as well as a combining power. . . . The Imagination can combine objects of sense into new forms, but it can do more than this. The objects of sense are, in most cases, merely the materials with which it works. The imagination is a plastic power, moulding the things of sense into new forms to express its ideals; and it is these ideals that constitute the real products of the imagination. The objects of the material world are to it like clay in the hands of the potter; it shapes them into forms according to its own ideals of grace and beauty. . . . He, who sees no more than a mere combination in these creations of the imagination, misses the essential element and elevates into significance that which is merely incidental."

Imagination, in some degree or phase, must come before voluntary physical action and conscious material creation. Everything that has been created by the hand of man has first been created in the *mind* of man by the exercise of the Imagination. Everything that man has wrought has first existed in his mind as an *ideal,* before his hands, or the hands of others, wrought it into material *reality.* As Maudsley says: "It is certain that in order to execute consciously a voluntary act we must have in the mind a conception of the aim and purpose of the act." Kay says: "It is as serving to guide and direct our various activities that mental images derive their chief value and importance. In anything that we purpose or intend to do, we must first of all have an idea or image of it in the mind, and the more clear and correct the image, the more accurately and efficiently will the purpose be carried out. We cannot exert an act of volition without having in the mind an idea or image of what we will to effect."

Upon the importance of a scientific use of the Imagination in every-day life, the best authorities agree. Maudsley says: "We cannot do an act voluntarily unless we know what we are going to do, and we cannot know exactly what we are going to do until we have taught ourselves to do it." Bain says: "By aiming at a new construction, we must clearly conceive what is aimed at. Where we have a very distinct and intelligible model before us, we are in a fair way to succeed; in proportion as the ideal is dim and wavering we stagger and miscarry." Kay says: "A clear and accurate idea of what we wish to do, and how it is to be effected, is of the utmost value and importance in all the affairs of life. A man's conduct naturally shapes itself according to the ideas in his mind, and nothing contributes more to his success in life than having a high ideal and keeping it constantly in view. Where such is the case one can hardly fail in attaining it. Numerous unexpected circumstances will be found to conspire to bring it about, and even what seemed at first hostile may be converted into means for its furtherance; while by having it constantly before the mind he will be ever ready to take advantage of any favoring circumstances that may present themselves."

Simpson says: "A passionate desire and an unwearied will can perform impossibilities, or what seem to be such, to the cold and feeble." Lytton says: "Dream, O youth, dream manfully and nobly, and thy dreams shall be prophets." Foster says: "It is wonderful how even the casualities of life seem to bow to a spirit that will not bow to them, and yield to subserve a design which they may, in their first apparent tendency, threaten to frustrate. When a firm decisive spirit is recognized it is curious to see how space clears around a man and leaves him room and freedom." Tanner says: "To believe firmly is almost tantamount in the end to accomplishment." Maudsley says: "Aspirations are often prophecies, the harbingers of what a man shall be in a condition to perform." Macaulay says: "It is related of Warren Hastings that when only seven years old there arose in his mind a scheme which through all the turns of his eventful life was never abandoned." Kay says: "When one is engaged in seeking for a thing, if he keep the image of it clearly before the mind, he will be very likely to find it, and that too, probably, where it would otherwise have escaped his notice." Burroughs says: "No one ever found the walking fern who did not have the walking fern in his mind. A person whose eye is full of Indian relics picks them up in every field he walks through. They are quickly recognized because the eye has been commissioned to find them."

Constructive Imagination differs from the phases of the faculty of Imagination which are akin to "Fancy," in a number of ways, the chief points of difference being as follows:

The Constructive Imagination is always exercised in the pursuance of *a definite intent and purpose.* The person so using the faculty starts out with the idea of accomplishing certain purposes, and with the direct intent of thinking and planning in that particular direction. The fanciful phase of the Imagination, on the contrary, starts with no definite intent or purpose, but proceeds along the line of mere idle phantasy or day-dreaming.

The Constructive Imagination *selects its material.* The person using the faculty in this manner abstracts from his general stock of mental images and impressions those particular materials which fit in with his general intent and purpose. Instead of allowing his imagination to wander around the entire field of memory, or representation, he deliberately and voluntarily selects and sets apart only such objects as seem to be conducive to his general design or plan, and which are logically associated with the same.

The Constructive Imagination operates upon the lines of *logical thought.* One so using the faculty subjects his mental images, or ideas, to his *thinking faculties,* and proceeds with his imaginative constructive work along the lines of Logical Thought. He goes through the processes of Abstraction, Generalization or Conception, Judgment and the higher phases of Reasoning, in connection with his general work of Constructive Imagination. Instead of having the objects of thought before him in material form, he has them represented to his mind *in ideal form*, and he works upon his material in that shape.

The Constructive Imagination is *voluntary* —under the control and direction of the will. Instead of being in the nature of a dream depending not upon the will or reason, it is directly controlled not only by reason but also by the will.

The Constructive Imagination, like every other faculty of the mind, may be developed and cultivated by Use and Nourishment. It must be exercised in order to develop its mental muscle; and it must be supplied with nourishment upon which it may grow. Drawing, Composing, Designing and Planning along any line is calculated to give to this faculty the exercise that it requires. The reading of the right kind of literature is also likely to lead the faculty into activity by inspiring it with ideals and inciting it by example.

The mind should be supplied with the proper material for the exercise of this faculty. As Halleck says: "Since the imagination has not the miraculous power necessary to create something out of nothing, the first essential thing is to get the proper perceptional material in proper quantity. If a child has enough blocks, he can build a castle or a palace. Give him but three blocks, and his power of combination is painfully limited. Some persons wonder why their imaginative power is no greater, when they have only a few accurate ideas.'' It thus follows that the active use of the Perceptive faculties will result in storing away a quantity of material, which, when represented or reproduced by the Memory, will give to the Constructive Imagination the material it requires with which to build. The greater the general knowledge of the person, the greater will be his store of material for this use. This knowledge need not necessarily be acquired at first hand from personal observation, but may also be in the nature of information acquired from the experience of others and known through their conversation, writings, etc.

The necessity of forming clear concepts is very apparent when we come to exercise the Constructive Imaginative. Unless we have clear-cut ideas of the various things concerned with the subject before us, we cannot focus the imagination clearly upon its task. The general ideas should be clearly understood and the classification should be intelligent. Particular things should be clearly seen in "the mind's eye;" that is, the power of visualization or forming mental images should be cultivated in this connection. One may improve this particular faculty by either writing a description of scenes or particular things we have seen, or else by verbally describing them to others. As Halleck says: "An attempt at a clear-cut oral description of something to another person will often impress ourselves and him with the fact that our mental images are hazy, and that the first step toward better description consists in improving them."

Tyndall has aptly stated the importance of visualizing one's ideas and particular concepts, as follows: "How, for example, are we to lay hold of the physical basis of light since, like that of life itself, it lies entirely without the domain of the senses? . . . Bring your imaginations once more into play and figure a series of sound-waves passing through air. Follow them up to their origin, and what do you there find? A definite, tangible, vibrating body. It may be the vocal chords of a human being, it may be an organ-pipe, or it may be a stretched string. Follow in the same manner a train of ether waves to their source, remembering at the same time that your ether is matter, dense, elastic and capable of motions subject to and determined by mechanical laws. What then do you expect to find as the source of a series of ether waves? Ask your imagination if it will accept a vibrating multiple proportion—a numerical ratio in a state of oscillation? I do not think it will. You cannot crown the edifice by this abstraction. The scientific imagination which is here authoritative, demands as the origin and cause of a series of ether waves a particle of vibrating matter quite as definite, though it may be excessively minute, as that which gives origin to a musical sound. Such a particle we name an atom or a molecule. I think the seeking intellect, when focused so as to give definition without penumbral haze, is sure to realize this image at the last."

By repeatedly exercising the faculty of Imagination upon a particular idea, we add power and clearness to that idea. This is but another example of the familar psychological principle expressed by Carpenter as follows: "The continued concentration of attention upon a certain idea gives it a dominant power." Kay says: "Clearness and accuracy of image is only to be obtained by repeatedly having it in the mind, or by repeated action of the faculty. Each repeated act of any of the faculties renders the mental image of it more clear and accurate than the preceding, and in proportion to the clearness and accuracy of the image will the act itself be performed easily, readily, skillfully. The course to be pursued, the point to be gained, the amount of effort to be put forth, become more and more clear to the mind. It is only from what we have done that we are able to judge what we can do, and understand how it is to be effected. When our ideas or conceptions of what we can do are not based on experience, they become fruitful sources of error."

Galton says: "There is no doubt as to the utility of the visualizing faculty where it is duly subordinated to the higher intellectual operations. A visual image is the most perfect form of mental representation wherever the shape, position and relation of objects in space are concerned. It is of importance in every handicraft and profession where design is required. The best workmen are those who visualize the whole of what they propose to do before they take a tool in their hands."

Kay says: "If we bear in mind that every sensation or idea must form an image in the mind before it can be perceived or understood, and that every act of volition is preceded by its image, it will be seen that images play an important part in all our mental operations. According to the nature of the ideas or images which he entertains will be the character and conduct of the man. The man tenacious of purpose is the man who holds tenaciously certain ideas; the flighty man is he who cannot keep one idea before him for any length of time, but constantly flits from one to another; the insane man is he who entertains insane ideas often, it may be, on only one or two subjects. We may distinguish two great classes of individuals according to the prevailing character of their images. There are those in whose mind sensory images predominate, and those whose images are chiefly such as tend to action. Those of the former class are observant, often thoughtful, men of judgment and, it may be, of learning; but if they have not also the active faculty in due force, they will fail in giving forth or in turning to proper account their knowledge or learning, and instances of this kind are by no means uncommon. The man, on the other hand, who has ever in his mind images of things to be done, is the man of action and enterprise. If he is not also an observant and thoughtful man, if his mind is backward in forming images of what is presented to it from without, he will be constantly liable to make mistakes."

Galton says of the faculty of visualization: "Our bookish and wordy education tends to repress this valuable gift of nature. A faculty that is of importance in all technical and artistic occupations, that gives accuracy to our perceptions and justness to our generalizations, is starved by lazy disuse, instead of being cultivated judiciously in such a way as will, on the whole, bring the best return. I believe that a serious study of the best method of developing and using this faculty without prejudice to the practice of abstract thought in symbols, is one of the many pressing desiderata in the yet unformed science of education.''

This consideration of the faculty of, and culture of, the Imagination, may appropriately be concluded by the following quotation from Prof. Halleck, which shows the danger of misuse and abuse of this important faculty. The aforesaid well-known authority says: ''From its very nature, the imagination is peculiarly liable to abuse. The common practices of day-dreaming or castle-building are both morally and physically unhealthful. We reach actual success in life by slow, weary steps. The day-dreamer attains eminence with one bound. He is without trouble a victorious general on a vast battlefield, an orator swaying thousands, a millionaire with every amusement at his command, a learned man confounding the wisest, a president, an emperor or a czar. After reveling in these imaginative sweets, the dry bread of actual toil becomes exceedingly distasteful. It is so much easier to live in regions where everything comes at the magic wand of fancy. Not infrequently these castle-builders abandon effort in an actual world. Success comes too slow for them. They become speculators or gamblers, and in spite of all their grand castles, gradually sink into utter nonentities in the world of action. . . . The young should never allow themselves to build any imaginative castle, unless they are willing by hard effort to try to make that castle a reality. They must be willing to take off their coats, go into the quarries of life, chisel out the blocks of the stone, and build them with much toil into the castle walls. If castle-building is merely the formation of an ideal, which we show by our effort that we are determined to attain, then all will be well."

It will be seen that, in reality, the Cultivation of the Imagination is rather the training and intelligent direction of that faculty, instead of the development of its power. The majority of people have the faculty of Imagination well developed, but to them it is largely an untrained, fanciful self-willed faculty. Cultivation is needed in the direction of bringing it under the guidance of the reason, and control by the will. Thought-Culture in general will do much for the Imagination, for the very processes employed in the development and cultivation of the various other faculties of the mind will also tend to bring the Imagination into subjection and under control, instead of allowing it to remain the wild, fanciful irresponsible faculty that it is in the majority of cases. Use the faculty of Imagination as a faculty of *Thought,* instead of a thing of *Fancy.* Attach it to the *Intellect* instead of to the *Emotions.* Harness it up with the other faculties of Thought, and your chariot of Understanding and Attainment will reach the goal far sooner than under the old arrangement. Establish harmony between Intellect and Imagination, and you largely increase the power and achievements of both.

FINIS.